# THE ANTIPHON

# THE ANTIPHON

*A Play*

DJUNA BARNES

FABER AND FABER

24 Russell Square

London

*First published in mcmlviii*
*by Faber and Faber Limited*
*24 Russell Square, London W.C.1*
*Printed in Great Britain by*
*Western Printing Services Limited, Bristol*

# CAUTIONARY NOTE

As a misreading of *The Antiphon* is not impossible, it might be well to keep in mind that Jack is breezy, not raffish; that Augusta is by turns timid and imperious; that Miranda, although indentured to ordeal, can rise to impassioned fury—but, never between the two women is there any sluttish whining. Their familiarity is their estrangement. They do not scold or bicker. Their duel is in hiatus, and should be waged with style.

AUGUST 1956                                                    D.B.

# PERSONS

The widow AUGUSTA BURLEY HOBBS
JONATHAN BURLEY, her brother
MIRANDA, her daughter
DUDLEY ⎱ her sons
ELISHA ⎰
'JACK BLOW', 'coachman'
Several travellers, on the way to port.


*Time*: During the war of 1939
*Place*: England, Burley Hall, in the township of Beewick,
formerly a college of chantry priests, in the Burley family
since the late seventeenth century.

# Act One

*To right and left, wide shallow steps leading to the gallery. Over the balustrade hang flags, gonfalons, bonnets, ribbons and all manner of stage costumes. Directly under the gallery, an arched doorway without a door. In the hall proper, a long table with a single settle facing front, at either end of which is set the half of a gryphon, once a car in a roundabout.*

*The table is laid in formal order, dominated by heavy candlesticks, a large tureen, a brass curfew bell, and a battered gilt mardi-gras crown.*

*To the left, standing before a paneless Gothic window, a dressmaker's dummy, in regimentals, surrounded by music stands, horns, fiddles, guncases, bandboxes, masks, toys and broken statues, man and beast.*

*To the right, through the tumbled wall, country can be seen, and part of a ruined colonnade. In the aperture, back view, a grey baize donkey, sitting.*

*MIRANDA, a tall woman in her late fifties, enters from the cloister. She has a distinguished but failing air, wearing an elegant but rusty costume, obviously of the theatre, a long cloak, buckled shoes and a dashing tricorne blowing with heron feathers. She favours her left side on a heavy headed cane.*

*She is followed, at a respectful distance, by JACK BLOW, a bearded fellow, of about the same age, wearing a patch. He is in high boots and long coachman's coat and carries a whip and creel. At his entrance he is holding his billycock straight up over his head, as though he expected applause from the gallery. His manner is racy.*

### MIRANDA
Here's a rip in nature; here's gross quiet,
Here's cloistered waste;
Here's rudeness once was home.

### JACK
There's no circulation in the theme . . .
The very fad of being's stopped . . .

7

MIRANDA

The wall is chapped where once the altar stood,
The basin dry, the music-stands in dust.
Horn and fiddle . . .

JACK

Mute as *Missae pro Defunctis.*
What prank of caution brought you back again?
Can no man imp himself his one life out,
And rest, becalmed in glory, like a flag,
Dismissed, but present?

MIRANDA

This field, this stay, this haunt of time, this mound,
This starting-post from which my mother ran . . .

JACK

It smells of hunting, like a widow's breath.

MIRANDA

Check well, Jack Blow, we leave it in the morning.
Then farewell this Benedictine shoe
That shod my mother's foot, and her dismay.

JACK

Truly. But where's your uncle Jonathan?
You said you came to kiss him fond farewell.
The scene is set but seems the actor gone.
No tither, weeper, wait or *cicerone*;
No beadle, bailiff, barrister, no clerk
In short no audience at all:
My hands will have to be your clamour, lady.

MIRANDA

Not so fast. It's true the webbed commune
Trawls up a wrack one term was absolute;
Yet corruption in its deft deploy
Unbolts the caution, and the vesper mole
Trots down the wintry pavement of the prophet's head.
In the proud flesh of the vanished eye
Vainglory, like a standing pool,

8

Invites the thirsty trades of paradise.
The world is cracked—but in the breach
My fathers mew.

JACK

Now that's a nip in zero that undoes me!
Who springs a trap, and it be not molested?

MIRANDA

When called his other name, whom heels the dog?
To what depths does one arise on hearing 'Love'?
This dated stumble, this running gig of days,
This dust that curries man and commons him—
This lichen bridled face of time. . .

JACK

Had Beewick not been on the way to port;
Had you not told me travellers afoot
Use Burley hall these days for shelter,
I'd have said avoid it.

MIRANDA

Would you?

JACK

[*Rolling his bowler down from his crook'd elbow to his palm*]
Well, there perhaps you have me;
This being, after all, your long loved England.

MIRANDA

This ruined address was once my mother's cot.
Here Augusta, that good woman, piped.
And if tradition and long tenancy,
In case however small be called the scale,
Keep and castle of the mind's dominion,
Say here upon a shield was diapered.
Tombs were her primers, cautions, sums;
Beewick her town, and Burley Hall her school.
Her spirit nested with the Tudor bat,
That sphincter rose that barnacled the groin

9

Of her hatched purpose; the very hub and rate
That kept the term of her diameter,
And held the proper of her inclination.


JACK
[*Rolling his hat back up his arm*]
Well! Aspired to aristocracy and glory?


MIRANDA
She so leaned on royalty and legend
She replaced herself as her own adversary,
Till she unstepped her claim, to gad oblivion,
And like a compass whirling without seat
Fell victim to a dial without hours—
Marriage to my father, and his folly.


JACK
I always said, there's not a pedestal
Won't shift its hero's bottom at some blow.
I myself, in my own boots, am fugitive.
There's nothing like destruction for an aim.
And here's its very pip.


MIRANDA
If that be so, good man, screw on this ruin,
And as the watchmaker his preying loupe debates
Mark you the pomp and practice of the ant.
Do all the conflating burdens of the wind
Disperse her apt and current hurry?


JACK
No.


MIRANDA
If, say, this afternoon the earth should quake
Sending a thousand flaggings stark upright,
Would not the canted beetle stick his mark?


JACK
Would he?

MIRANDA

And on the dial's dislocated time
Wind up his purpose?

JACK

Why, I think it so.

MIRANDA

Yet here Augusta, my poor mother, tipped
The comely balance of her country state
To the staggered compass of barbarian—
My father, Titus Higby Hobbs of Salem—

JACK

She who once hung swinging on a gate . . .

MIRANDA

Boating the hedges with her open hand,
Peering down the lanes for visitors;
Striking back at springtime, like a kid
Hopping and skipping to the summer's day;
Bawling and baaing out her natural glee
With such an host of ignorant visions fed
She but peeped about with gladness, just to hark
'Sleeper awake!' and ran on 'katy-dids'—

JACK

An insect not indigenous—

MIRANDA

With that mistake you have the tragedy.
Harnessed to spring, and lisping on the bit,
A long wind playing out her cast of hair,
She came singing and hopping, when in one
Scant scything instant was gaffed down.
Lying still as water in a stick
That carpenters do level with,
All backward in a flail of locks went to,
With cobalt eye in passion's clabber drowned,
Holding a single flower upright.

JACK

God's mercy!

MIRANDA

Thus, puddled public as the stable-fly
Performing the tragic ballet on her back,
She swarmed the impacted seasons with offence,
And of that marriage pupped truncated grief,
As women must who mother discontent,
And any dream come short.

JACK

And you the arms and legs of it!

MIRANDA

Of that luckless sprawl, three sons she leaned to fairly:
On me she cast the privy look of dogs
Who turn to quiz the thing they've dropped.
Yet in her hour, become by me, twice headed,
The one head on the other stared, and wept.

JACK

[With a long whistle]
What a ferocious travel is your mind!
How then do you find this term of silence?

MIRANDA

Most moved. It is not well to be so moved
In lost familiarity—

                                        And I fear merchants.

JACK

Look—
Don't turn me roundabout, but tell me squarely
How did your father get here anyway?

MIRANDA

Why, grandmother brought him in, from Middletown,
And set him on her perch in Grosvenor Square.

JACK

[With mock astonishment]
No! Trotting up on culture, brief in hand,

12

His horse shot under him at forty-five degrees!
O the dreadful moves of vanity!


MIRANDA

Say less, Jack Blow, for knowing nothing of it.


JACK

I'd say more, for the very same default.
For who is wiser than the total stranger?
Have I not the picture of the man?
In every quarter of his disposition
Complete perfection sat!


MIRANDA

You talk too much, too much include,
Too much leave out.


JACK

In my mind's gallery he sits entire;
In tip-top belly-leather, watch-swag swinging
At his bulk, like ferry chains on docks.
Stickler for the freedom of the sexes,
There ranged behind his easy seated bum,
Fearfully detained, and standing up.
(You've told me he believed in Brigham Young)
His pack of wives, in Concord cameos,
Flushed out in tabby, chatelaines and bugles,
Their bustles close upon them, like a grudge;
Flanked by warming-pans, bassoons and bastards.


MIRANDA

One would almost say you knew the man.


JACK

I wander where men walk; remember, lady?
I found you, a pilgrim, in the way.


MIRANDA

I thank you for it, let that be enough:
Therefore, lock down the windows, shut the doors.

13

JACK

Pull up the walls, saw down the wind, scoop up the sea!
Strut back the bridge, lock up the stars and sky!
Lady, be not such a party to yourself;
Do not abuse your present expectation
With such an haggard look.
If you propose, by bolting up the air,
To manacle perdition—
    [*Humming*]
                        'Hey, then who
'Passes by this road so late,
'Always gay.'

MIRANDA

I've told you—I fear merchants.

JACK

Merchants, merchants, merchants!
Ten forty times you've muttered merchants!
What merchants? Moslems? traders—
    [*Pulling at his chin*]
Stroking their abominable amber—
Greedy landlord to outchambered flies?
Or would it be
A Lama, swaddled up in buzzard grey,
Seeding a stopped watch of its hours?
Or something nearer home?

MIRANDA

Enough—enough.

JACK

    [*Finger to the side of his nose*]
Brothers? with their ticker tapes and totals?
Or worser yet perhaps, your widowed mother
Checking up on what is not her business?

MIRANDA

    [*Turning straight around upon him*]
Starve your tongue, Jack Blow, be still—
I fear brothers.

14

JACK

[*Swinging his whip*]
But not your mother? What?
O meridian of ague, how you wane,
Your finger ring being tumbled to the joint.
Slow scampering time has picked the locks,
And of your credit thrown the key away!
Still you fare forward, hapless voyager—
I think you've told me something short.

MIRANDA

Assume the mischief.

JACK

Mischief Madame! I expect to be,
In this knock-about of general war,
Up to my neck in steeples; starting stoats,
Hens in hats, and sailing ships in lanes.
And by the edging off of custom, get me bit
By grounded gargoyles that once staled the sky
With rash Orion's water. Mischief lady?
I expect to see myopic conquerors
With pebbled monocles and rowel'd heels,
In a damned and horrid clutch of vagrancy
Dredging the Seine of our inheritance;
Or dragging from the Tiber and the Thames
Cruppers, bridles, bits and casket handles;
Rocking-horses and sabres from the fair—
Trawling the Hellespont for log and legend
And all things whatsoever out of grasp.
But, to get us back to *terra firma*—

MIRANDA

Who *are* you, Jack Blow?

JACK

At the moment I haven't the faintest notion.
As I was saying—

MIRANDA

[*Listening*] Psst! I hear something!

15

JACK

They say a snail from Caesar's grave
Crawled into Napoleon's snuff-box.

MIRANDA

Where are we, indeed, that we are only here?

JACK

Let us say that presently we haunt.
Would oiling thrushes get them through a sieve?
Nay, rigour does it. Who has a right to rigour?

MIRANDA

Miranda has.

JACK

                        Then go brace it, girl.

MIRANDA

I'll go to the back, and see what I may see.
Let no one in.

                                                        [*Exit*]

JACK

Let no one in? The very air is out.
Now there's one whose look is heavy with escape!
  [*He goes up to inspect the table. He lifts the cover of the tureen, sticking
  his finger in.*]
*Bouillabaisse?* That tussle of the sea?
Aii! Steep as the upper lip of Finnegan!
  [*He replaces the cover nervously, sensing he is not alone*]
Ah, well, being October, and my shilling lean,
I'll thrive in vacancy—
  [*The brothers appear,* DUDLEY *at the window,* ELISHA *on the gallery,
  unseen, but sensed by* JACK]
But—I do not like a feast where dogs lie still.
  [JACK *moves around to the head of the table and stands before the
  winged half of the gryphon*]
I've seen a judge
Sitting in the credit of his chair,
So abandon justice that his ears
Stood, in abdication, on his head.

16

Yet did the astounded air gag up the verdict?
It did not.
   [*Pretending a nonchalance he does not feel, sings, under his breath*]
'Who passes by this road so late—'
They say soliloquy is out of fashion,
It being a kind of talking to your betters.
   [*He climbs into the chair*]
But then what motion but betrays oneself?
Esau's heel trips every man his running.
But Jack—not running—disinherited?
Do I move under, like the pilot-fish?
Am I a cow-bird, shill, or Judas goat,
Gaited to walk on other people's pools
As the skating-fly who skips on sleeping water?
Or do I, by some private irritation
Set about to step on my own rope?
Do I unplot my head by plucking hairs?
Or throw my lines away between my teeth?
Or do I so entirely slip from custom
That I sprawl in any place, a king?
Why then, so be it.
If crouching on a throne's called sitting
I'll sit this out.
   [*He stiffens, hearing a noise in the gallery; but does not turn*]
Do I hear the world approaching at my back?
Then though the world be present, I'll be proctor—
   [*With increasing bravado, calling, like a barker*]
Hurry! Hurry! This way for the toymen:
This way, strutters, for the bearded lady;
The human skeleton, the fussy dwarf,
The fat girl with a planet in her lap;
The swallower of swords whose hidden lunge
Has not brought up his adversary yet!
   [JONATHAN BURLEY, *an old man, and slight, enters from a door under
   the gallery.* DUDLEY *and* ELISHA *dodge out of sight.*]

BURLEY

Good evening.

JACK
   The devil!

B                          17

BURLEY

At your service.

JACK

Bless me, I thought I had advantage here.

BURLEY

A not uncommon misapprehension, sir.

JACK

*Who* was that woman?

BURLEY

What woman?

JACK

You must have seen her.
She went out as you came in.

BURLEY

My dear sir, many come and go.
Since the war, this has been a refuge
For every person out of keys.
    [*With hint of irony*]
In other words, a kind of Hampton Court
For gentle folk—afoot.

JACK

Is this not that sometime Burley seat
Since the early something seventeen,
That I hear referred to, metaphorically,
As 'The Abbey'?

BURLEY

Quite.

JACK

College of chantry priests, more properly?

BURLEY

Formerly.

JACK

Well then, good fellow, be not sly with me.
This being open house, be open also.
Was that not Miranda, late of Burley?

BURLEY

Late? She visits often. As you see,
She leaves her bonnets, flags and boxes,
She's fond of carnivals and all processions.
Might I ask you, did you come by horse?

JACK

Horse it was, and carriage. I hear Titus Hobbs
(The Lady's father, whom you may recall)
Once rode horseback, through this very lobby;
Up one bank of steps and down the other,
Like a bloody Gascon.

BURLEY

He did indeed.

JACK

Well, I'm lesser—I tied mine to a tree.

BURLEY

Come, I'll give you a hand.

JACK

Hand? What for?

BURLEY

Your luggage. Surely you have brought your luggage?

JACK

Why, yes, to a shaving—

BURLEY

Then come with me.

JACK

Wait a minute. Are you steward?

BURLEY

In a way of speaking.

JACK
Long?

BURLEY

Very. All my life.

JACK

Then I'll tell you, this luggage that you mention,
Could it be, good sir, or could it not,
A beast-box, say, a doll's house, or an Ark?
[*Aside*]
Now am I a well made fool!
[*Aloud*]
An unholy covenant, a contract,
Sealed by the jaw-bone of an ass?

BURLEY

I do not follow you.

JACK
[*Preparing to go with* BURLEY]

I follow *you*, but not now for the box.
I would my horse might be attended somewhat;
Starving, sir, as all the world is.

[*Exeunt* BURLEY *and* JACK]
[DUDLEY *steps in through the window*, ELISHA *through the door.*
DUDLEY *is the elder of the two, very much the executive, heavily set,
chewing on a cigar, still wearing his hat and carrying his umbrella,
open. In his left hand he holds a large gold watch, chain dangling. He
meets* ELISHA *in the middle of the hall*, ELISHA *diligently strewing
almond shells as he comes.* ELISHA *is younger and on the smarter side.*]

ELISHA

What do you make of it?

DUDLEY
[*Turning slowly, in one piece*]
A beastly brawl in nature; broken Greeks;

20

An orchestra, decamped, and petticoats.
A blasted donkey, and a baby's ball.
    [*He kicks it*]
In short, when I don't understand a thing—
Stand back—I kick it!

ELISHA
    [*Following the example, kicking a fallen statue*]
When I see a thing I cannot rate,
I rate it.
Why did mother speak Beewick so high?


DUDLEY
The strangers, who are they?
That old man, and that hanky-panky fellow?
Somehow I had failed to count on company,
Except for sightseers, every other Friday.


ELISHA
Every other day, and not this day?


DUDLEY
I'd simply not counted on accompanied Miranda,
And I don't know why. Here's fox-earth.


ELISHA
And not a sign of brother Jeremy.
And just as well—he had wild fits of clemency.


DUDLEY
Who is man that he should stand down wind?


ELISHA
That's not the point, the point is sister;
And that *was* Miranda, by her back, or was it?
Everything's a little out of context.


DUDLEY
Our deadly beloved vixen, in the flesh.
What more could we want?

ELISHA

Less of her self-possession—and her vagrancy
That in a wink she makes nine points of law.
There's nothing to be gained befriending that one;
So I say, let's have no sentiment.


DUDLEY

You've lost the stirrup—who said anything of sentiment?
But that old man could he be bribed?


ELISHA

   [*Cracking a nut*]
I doubt it. A saying has it—
Each man in the other man, his eye,
Rides game, and hunting up-side-down
Grapples his spectre to his ghost;
You won't tear that one from himself.


DUDLEY

The old retainer all tied up in custom.
You know, sometime Mother and Miranda
Are so entirely breezed up by the Mighty
That if I saw myself, backward, in their mirror,
I'm not so sure what sort of beast I'd see.


ELISHA

Turn them to the wall, the mirrors blank.
What else, dear boy?


DUDLEY

What else?
Here am I, watchmaker to the world,
Master of a more than thousand souls,
Yet what of me does that leave when I whistle?


ELISHA

One thousand mice.


DUDLEY

Precisely. So I'll tell you what I wish:

I wish I'd built a mouse-trap, bigger than Creation,
And caught myself—as Master and the Man.

ELISHA

Is it possible we're father's blasphemy?

DUDLEY

By my God—I wonder.

ELISHA

What, dear boy?

DUDLEY

Do all old women have a savage death?

ELISHA

Well, I always say that dog eats dog.
Why are you holding up that tell-tale watch?
Remember, we are marvellous clever fellows.

DUDLEY

Timing.

ELISHA

Timing? What time have you?

DUDLEY

Borrowed.
Mother will come in at any moment—
She can't sleep forever in the car—
And Miranda isn't far away.

ELISHA

And obviously out of patron and of money.

DUDLEY

We'll never have so good a chance again;
Never, never such a barren spot,
Nor never again such anonymity as war.
All old people die of death, remember?
We're strangers here; they people that estrangement.

Good, here's innocence, let's taste it.
Landscapes alter everything. The sea
Will wash us. Monday we were men, but Tuesday?
Undaunted! Swing in my stability.
The ground they stand on, let's uncover it,
Let us pull their shadows out from under them!

ELISHA

But Jeremy, who has the favour of their love
And can be kind, where's he? Where's Jeremy?
[*Hearing the approach of* BURLEY *and* JACK, DUDLEY *and* ELISHA
*dodge out of sight.*]

JACK

Now for dinner!

BURLEY

First, sir, I must ask you for credentials.

JACK

Credentials? What, in a bare-faced open forum?
This is nothing short of black suspicion.

BURLEY

Perhaps. But I ask where from, where going?

JACK

O underwriter!
Would you that I spell it?

BURLEY

I would.

JACK

Can I say, that from an unseen perch,
A feather's fallen from the air, and I have caught it?

BURLEY

No.

JACK

No?
But to tell you, fret by fret, would wear you.

24

Therefore call me Tom-O-Bedlam, Lantern Jack;
We are the look-outs of the fear blue city Paris—
Orphans of the war.

BURLEY

Less skipping, if you please.

JACK

Suspect *her* as member of the Odeon—
A dresser to the opera—and say, for tragedy,
Swept the Comédie Française! Me?
Plain Jack—who followed close behind,
The whipper-in.

BURLEY

Courtesy requires that when you speak,
You make it more than silence.

JACK

Now there's a comely but demanding argument!
We're sailing in the morning.

BURLEY

Are you Miranda's friend?

JACK

                Friend?

BURLEY

Where did you meet her, sir?

JACK

I said I followed—but let us now to dinner!

BURLEY

A moment. Perhaps it's best I tell you who I am.
I am, sir, Jonathan of Burley, steward;
Miranda's uncle.

JACK

Bless us! Studied for the ministry,
That one, and didn't make it?

25

That one.

She told me of you, all the way from Dover;
A truly soaring high opinion, too.

You met her in *Dover*?

Wait. Say I fell in a time ago in Paris.
I, with the single, she, the compound eye
Met back to back—a kind of paradox.
Descending the terraces of Sacré Cœur
I saw her stand before the city literal,
Tall, withdrawn, intent and nothing cunning;
Incorporate with the air, and more than still,
Her hands dropped and thoroughly performed—
The lost tension one notes in tragediennes
Who've left the tragic gesture to the stage,
And so go forth alone to meet disaster.
Then said I to me, in fit declaim,
'Lord, excellence and fierce vulgarity
So overlap this last hour of the world,
She's forsaking covert for some prowl,
As the leopard in a land made desolate.'

Shall we get on with it?

It can't be halted, as I'm well aware.
My ash-plant, on its own, began to beat
Like a rod possessed, and barking into bloom
Went tapping in her footsteps, one on one.
Now I am he who knows that Lucifer
Not only fell, but came down bunged in stars.

You do?

#### JACK

I do.
I said she hears trapped silence, or I much mistake
The thunder on the anvil of the ear.
Say we met in parting—on the drum's first rouse.

#### BURLEY

But your rig in Dover?

#### JACK

Say I have a horse in every port—and say
I saw a pilgrim, wandering and walking.

#### BURLEY

And half-way hard on Beewick—caught her?

#### JACK

Half-way home I caught her, if you say so.
From the Sacré Cœur down to the lower city.
Strict headed horses of the Garde Republicaine,
In dark rank flew prancing all before us,
Drilling out a reek of cobbles, as an iron
Plunging in a quarry reeks out stone.
Tails that once had catered to the buttocks' foss
Now flew the helmets of the haughty riders,
Rushing past the hospice yard, where little men
Beneath stone effigies, weighed down in birds
Smoked black cigars, while on the balconies
The patients, clock-wise, practised their recovery.

#### BURLEY

I see—or do I?

#### JACK

You've made it in one. Thus we went down together,
Down to the markets of the Avénue du Maine.

#### BURLEY

Why?

#### JACK

Why? Trade being over, and the push-carts gone

One can chart the public privacy
Of wretched destitution. See how each soul
Without enough to live on—too much to die—
Drags its country and its bedroom on a string:
Each in a rusty gown, that in an age
Comes to style again without its notice;
Its head thrown up on its shovel-bonnet,
The galled check-reins of velvet bearding the chin
With shaking bows. So unsolicited of anything,
It bobs rejection with every palsied nod,
Its every taken breath drawn as emetic—
Pushing an empty carriage, where its infant
Nothing lies.

BURLEY

Why all this?

JACK

O literal of mind! O earth-bound checker!
You'd snap a rubber band around an eagle!
Miranda was going backward through her target,
Her face set grim for Beewick:
This was part of that company.

BURLEY

[*To himself*]

Fantastick—Scapin!

[*To* JACK]

You should have been an actor.

JACK

I was, I am, the company unseen;
I think they call it 'carrying the spear'.

BURLEY

So Miranda leaned against the Gate of Punishment
And looked?

JACK

Not yet, not then; she had stops to make—
[*Hearing a noise*]

Someone about?

The wind. A traveller—

                        Traveller? Not now, not tonight, I hope.

One or two perhaps, before the morning.

There being more things on earth than we have dreamed of?
Good. So, raising up my billycock in air
I cried—extempore—'This must be the day!'
And was about to leap into its breach
With, 'Lady, Dame confounded, Madame, hey!'—
Being vertical is one of her positions—
And toppling where she lies one of her stations—
When she was off, and such a look she had,
I can assure you, froze me to the heel.
Then ping! We're in the middle of a party
All hung around with fireflies and with lanterns—
Foxglove, harebell, and in the pulpit, Jack;
A *bahnhof*, Waterloo, Grand Central Station,
A terminal for tea, and no trains running;
A ministry of protocol, a Rumpelmayer,
The very top *haut ton* of everything.
And bowling through, old beasties bobbed and bibbed.
Some hidden by a hedge of paper roses,
Some with their chips down, like the mighty blind
Playing silence on an higher level, found it,
Tapping the long tooth with a leather fan.
Others, in the dark rehearsal of climacteric
Held back the fading crescent of eclipse,
Turning the eye-ball to the bitter dark.
But for my soul, I could not date the day.

It would seem to me Miranda's private hour.
Were you welcome?

Welcome? Bless you, sir, I'm well past welcome:

Of man's despairs we've had the deal and dole.
This was Miranda's public, her herd in hobble;
Her once-upon-a-time; her court, her people;
Her bleak-of-spirit, and her consternation
For she is one who knows that man is prouder
Of his fame than of the way he made it.
Knowing nothing now is wrought by hand
To give into the hand particular,
Nor pride of execution.

Then came the footmen, with the cakes and ices?

Then came the flunkies with the tea and tarts.
I never saw so many famished O's
Gulping as their gape depended on it.
Pasties there were, in every form and fancy.
(Woman's last love always ends in batter
In the semblance of some local 'nob',
Or some monstrous windy senator.)
So there they were, kickshaws *au miel, montée,*
Laced down with *menthe,* with *aquavit* and rum,
Strolled about with sorgum and with treacle;
Almonds, salted, chestnuts, glazed, and jellies—
Compotes, marchpane, apricots and figs—
And every mould an image to the life,
Of whatsoever party fame was killing.

[*Nervously striking one closed hand into the other*]
*Then* you made your move?

No. Too near the famish. Those who realized
That present speed was making obsolete
Their very memory, or any term to tell it—
Such were trying to get into the act, by panting.
*Holinight!* what a powdered smoke of sugar 'rose
Making confections of the dowagers and dandies!

When, zut! Miranda and the old *Belle Laide* of Langue d'Oc—
The one who'd roiled the bowels of the bank
To such effect, at ninety-one she stood
Stiff as a hitching-post, and neighing diamonds—
Met face to face.

BURLEY

Did you say of Langue d'Oc?

JACK

            I said it.

BURLEY

Bless my soul! That must have been my sister
Elvira—one Burley got herself to France.
Did she sit it out?

JACK

In a slashing zone of taffeta, she did.
Her head, gabled in a cone of voile, was caught
In a mesh that wove the face away,
Curbing the waspish bodkin of her eyes,
Sparkling with the fornications of the mint.

BURLEY

*Now* you made your move.

JACK

Tut! Tut! The trigger finger of both hands were numb
From thumbing down the runaway of ages.
This ancient of nights, all rigging and dead heat
Made carbon of her gems, and oxides of her metals.
Yet now, upon the changing of the spirits' guards,
Spoke in tones stentorian, a smother
Like Field-Marshal, head-down in a cistern,
A grand *savate* to the middle air,
Where do inhabit troops of possibilities.

BURLEY

Come, come, good man, I know as well as any
The lily, onion and confessional

31

Have many layers. Pare on, acquaint me.
This life is not the first encounter, sir.

JACK

Would you have me tell of dedication
Dead-pan, tight-lipped, minced, and orthodox?
Or will you have this forthright?

BURLEY

Forthright.

JACK

[*In a stage whisper*]
I'm not too sure what's brewing hereabouts.

BURLEY

[*Starting*] Eh?

JACK

No. But 'fore God, abet me,
That I not default. Now, then, where was I?

BURLEY

Just up to the point where Elvira—

JACK

So I was. Her hip well stapled back, the thigh
In its cup full quartered, lay and couched
Where she sat checking on her gap in time—
In one hand she held her bracelets up,
Loose on the bone.

BURLEY

Weighing the rate of her departure.

JACK

Exactly.
Posting finger high, I cried out 'Olé!
At the apex, lady, do not scream.'

BURLEY

To whom?

Miranda. '*The croupier* is raking in,' I said. 'Ignore it.
We're all at profile in this session, girl—
    [DUDLEY *and* ELISHA *begin to close in, moving sideways as children
    in a game of tag, unseen by* JACK, *seen by* BURLEY]
And orphaned on both sides, it's in the plot.
But you, or I mistake my cyclone-lamp,
Are headed for nobility of one.
An advantage, some there are who say
Of thirty years, providing you are royal.
Failing that, why *lento, lento*, lady;
You must learn to buckle to extremity;
Fall face-down upon a field Tiepolo—
Even though it is upon the ceiling.
Whip up your splendours and your consternations,
Bank to performance; give tongue for tongue,
Stand to the trumpets and the terrors,
For all the tapestries have thrown their spears!'

BURLEY

All that?

JACK

Entire.
I did believe that day all boisterous hell
Was loosed: I tell you that you be informed—
I take it you're her last of Burley.
That day I made such haste I met myself;
I knew I looked on launched catastrophe.
So, cracking in the middle of my flurry
I cried, 'Mass, mass, piano and piano!'
What else can one, who sees perform its absence
So stark a soul, at such a rate, but keep
One hand above the other gasping, 'Presto!'
What do you make of it?

BURLEY

Nothing.

JACK

And that's precisely why Jack Blow came running,
Swallowing himself and muttering

'Will Miranda reach the weir upright?' And will she,
Being such an upland play? I tell you
That you, who have not seen her many years,
May be the wiser.

BURLEY

Of late I've seen her often.
[*Inadvertently the* BROTHERS *make a noise.*]

JACK

Halt! What's that?

BURLEY

[*His eyes fixed on the* BROTHERS]
Nothing. Travellers—

JACK

Probably a something worse.
I wondered, will she recover from the stroke
That felled her at her people's gate, a life ago?
So I watched as for a while she stood,
The seven choice bones of her neck down-turned,
The tall plumed turret of her hat becalmed.
Thus the aquiline regard of two worlds met:
'Someone owes a cock to Aesculapius,' she said.
That moment I became her man—
Out of the high fear.

BURLEY

Then you will betray her.

JACK

It won't be necessary; she is her own collision.
She walks like majesty, but is a bumpkin.
She has rash fortitude; she will undo herself,
Meeting herself but totally unarmed.
Therefore, let us begin it.

[*At the same moment that* MIRANDA *appears on the gallery,* DUDLEY
*and* ELISHA, *without further caution, move forward.* ELISHA *leans,
still cracking almonds, against the lay-figure, while* DUDLEY, *hat still*

34

*on, umbrella up, sits in the chair at the head of the table, his feet braced against its top.*]

JACK

[*Without too much surprise*] What have we here?

MIRANDA

[*On the balcony, softly striking the heel of her hand upon the balustrade, speaking under her breath as she hears the faint approaching sound of the tapping of a ferule on the flagging*]
No, no, no, no, no, no!

CURTAIN

# Act Two

SAME AS ACT ONE. PERSONS IN SAME POSITION.

[*The widow* AUGUSTA BURLEY HOBBS, *gaunt, determined, dressed in the legal severity of long black; collared and cuffed in spotless linen, comes on from the colonnade, tapping the paving with the ferule of her umbrella, more for emphasis than caution.*]

AUGUSTA

Why was I left to drowse my coming home?
So then, I'm in my father's house again!
Who said I must be present? He did
Jeremy my son—where is he?

DUDLEY

Hi there mother!

BURLEY

Welcome.

AUGUSTA

[*Peering about*]
My plan is subtler than to mourn
The horrid wrack of Burley standing down;
I'm my own habit yet, and take to sitting—
Shall I know him when I see him?
[*Noticing her daughter on the balcony*]
Ah, how are you old, Miranda?

MIRANDA

Being apt.

AUGUSTA

Now that we're here, all but the one, a chair!

BURLEY

[*Hurriedly turning the prow end of the gryphon*]
At once! Immediately!

36

AUGUSTA

[*Seating herself*]
Thank you, I hold no brief for standing.
As I came up the terraces of Beewick,
Looking about to see how Beewick stands,
I saw the gables raining down their rooks
In such a belching squall, I cried 'God's mercy,
I do believe they're throwing birds away!
Or could it be there's funeral in air?

BURLEY

Have you transacted birds?

AUGUSTA
Certainly not!

BURLEY

They hang upon the finger like a gage,
Thrown down of an unseen adversary;
Suddenly you're prisoner of space;
And like St. Francis' fist, hemmed up in flight.

AUGUSTA

[*Attentively*]
It's terrible to come on high ghostly things
When one is old and ravelled to the ground.
I pushed four children from my list and yet
One stayed in the web to pull it down
But enough of that. I see no horse nor hen,
Nor happy squire standing on his turf.
What wild suppers must the squirrels eat
Who find their harvest such a scattered game.

BURLEY

This Jeremy?

AUGUSTA

Though he put me out to pasture, that same son
Has called me back to Beewick and to England.
He should be here, considering he left me.

37

#### DUDLEY

Half a lifetime since, to be correct.


#### AUGUSTA

[*Searching her pocket*]
I have his letter here—now where is it? Don't tell me
I have lost—mislaid my son—I had it.
        [*Noticing the chair she is sitting on*]
Isn't this the beast I sat upon
Staring at his father—that dead man?


#### BURLEY

Rest.


#### AUGUSTA

Old man, where I sit, I rotted out such play
Was to have been a fort.
        [*Seeing the curfew-bell*]
Ah, the curfew-bell of cousin Pegamont!
He used to ring it over barley broth
To call his needy pensioners—a charity
He watered like an horse.


#### BURLEY

Come, come, he was a gentle fellow;
Though even as a child so Attic salt
The nurse refused to change him without gloves.


#### AUGUSTA

Then you knew my cousin Pegamont?
        [*To her sons*]
He locked the turnkey up, with his own iron.
Best carpenter in Burley. What a craftsman!
Set up his own roof-tree. It can be said that no man
Has a home, who has not smelled his scaffold.


#### BURLEY

Precisely.


#### AUGUSTA

Where now that honour in the hand? I told my sons
All the silver spoons were swallowed.

ELISHA

Hardly cricket, what?

AUGUSTA

Don't behave as though you'd never travelled—
Though it's true, you haven't.
    [*To* JACK]
Who are you, boy?

JACK

Plain Jack—juggler.

AUGUSTA

    [*Turning to* BURLEY]
A good scant face. Do I know it?

BURLEY

Your brother Jonathan.

AUGUSTA

    [*With a slight scream*]
Jonathan! My very altered brother—
How am I glad to see you!
I came the long way out to find my home,
My brother, and my son, the wanderer.
Have you seen Jeremy?

BURLEY

I don't think so.

AUGUSTA

I find my cradle, unlike the rocking-stone
That recovers quickly when it's pushed,
Rocked out of date. I find my brother's hairs
Fallen to their valance; my dear son?
I find him not at all.

BURLEY

Give him time.

AUGUSTA

It's strange that he has sent for me all on a sudden,

39

Who have not seen him twenty years.
And by those twenty years twice twenty stranger;
I dread my sons, and love them bitterly.
    [*Recollecting herself*]
But what am I about, not made you known—
Jonathan—I see you know my daughter—
This is Dudley, manufacturer of clocks—

DUDLEY
             Watches.

JACK
'The king was in his counting house—'

ELISHA
[*Spitting out shells*] Touché!

AUGUSTA
Both of them, as you observe, successful—
    [*To* ELISHA]
And stop bleating!
Jonathan, this Elisha, Dudley's publicist.

ELISHA
Hi!

AUGUSTA
They say, in short, it's why they came this way—
I could have managed all alone for Jeremy.
And what does Jeremy?—

ELISHA
Everything—including Moldavian muscatel—

AUGUSTA
[*Ignoring this with contemptuous pity*]
Children, my brother Jonathan.

BURLEY
Welcome, gentlemen, and prosper you.
40

MIRANDA

Be each other's creatures cautiously.

AUGUSTA

Knowing my daughter, what think of her?

BURLEY

I think her as I know her.

JACK

How does she stand?

BURLEY

Complete.

AUGUSTA

[*Appraising Jack*]
My good man, who are you?

JACK

A friend.

AUGUSTA

Friend?

JACK

In trust.

AUGUSTA

Jonathan was my favourite brother—

BURLEY

[*With troubled modesty*]

No, no.

AUGUSTA

Studied for the ministry—

BURLEY

Glad to settle for the stewardship of Burley.

41

AUGUSTA

Truly, a master of the organ—

BURLEY

Ah, that's a long, long time ago.

AUGUSTA

How are our people, Jonathan?

BURLEY

Alas, my dear Augusta.

AUGUSTA

I feared it. As I came up to Burley
I saw no faces that I saw—
[*To* ELISHA]
Elisha, stop it! Stop cracking nuts!
[*To* DUDLEY]
Put the umbrella down, you're not that out of doors!

BURLEY

There are aunts somewhere, and uncles doubtlessly—

AUGUSTA

Nephews and nieces? Do you live in the house?

BURLEY

No, for the present in the village.

AUGUSTA

Who brings you tea?

BURLEY
[*Dense in regard to the suggestion*]
Sometimes my boy brings a pot of ale;
Sometimes, in the butler's pantry, tea—
The pantry's still intact.

AUGUSTA
[*Sweeping the formal arrangement of the table with pleased eye*]
The table—just as it used to be.

42

BURLEY
                    For custom's sake.


AUGUSTA
My husband, Titus, sitting at that end
Gobbled like a turkey.


BURLEY
                    Like usurper.


AUGUSTA
I such a prudent, such a country girl!


BURLEY
                    But?


AUGUSTA
I thought to be the mother of Aristocrats
And got me what? Three boys in trades, and one—


DUDLEY
                    Gosling, on the loose.
[*There is a noise off-stage of people passing.*]


AUGUSTA
Heavens, what is that?


BURLEY
Nothing, strangers, passing—a ship leaves in the morning.


AUGUSTA
        [*Still somewhat apprehensive*]
Do you presume it possible his mistresses
Still roam the countryside? I almost wish
The creatures walked again, I'd have a fourth at bridge—
But I was coming to Miranda—

    *

DUDLEY
Behold Miranda! In the zodiac
She stands for Virgo—just for laughs in heaven.

43

BURLEY

Don't you like your sister?

DUDLEY

Dear uncle, we adore her, in the highest—

ELISHA

But to know her is extravagance—so British!

AUGUSTA

Pay no attention to my boys, they ape their father,
Who looked down on the British with the utmost envy.
I'd hoped my children would have shone in manners,
And Miranda come in terrible with honours.

BURLEY

And did she?

DUDLEY

Mother thought to knock a queen down with her broom—
She, with the peerage in her pocket,
Father, with Josh Billings in his boot!

ELISHA

I hear Miranda's all get-out in France
And apparently a scrivener in England.

BURLEY

She is praised here and across the channel,
She's particularly welcome here in Beewick.

DUDLEY

Beewick's a little place—no credit in New York.

AUGUSTA

Jonathan, forgive my sons their malice,
It comes of being the first time over-water—
They're out of custom; let us then to fortunes.
Now where are my cards?

JACK

Cards in Carthage!

44

AUGUSTA

Why not cards in Carthage? No? Then chess.

BURLEY

Chess? A strategy
To keep two solemn dead men sitting up.

AUGUSTA

[*A spool of twist falls from her pocket as she searches for her cards*]
Ah my bones and bobbins!
[*The spool rolls out of sight*]
I used to make me laces, Jonathan,
To keep from sulking over worser matters.
[*Sighs*]
For lace? No journey it adapts to;
For people? No journey brings them home.
[*The spool rolls back into the hall*]
Gracious, someone *is* about!

BURLEY

Children—pilgrims—on the way to port—
I regret I've nothing here to lift the spirit.

AUGUSTA

You know I never touch a thing!

BURLEY

My dear Augusta, I know nothing.

AUGUSTA

But I starve!

BURLEY

[*Hastily*]
Let's see what we can do for that.

AUGUSTA

[*Anxiously*]
No, no, don't move.

45

ELISHA
[*Clapping the carnival crown upon his head*]
'The Queen was playing cards, with the Bishop of Limoges—'

DUDLEY
But she found 'the cupboard bare—'

AUGUSTA
They always play the fool; pay no attention—
Eh, there's the wind again, someone *is* prowling.
I've said I sometimes wish my husband's hussies
Walked again; in time the mind forgets
What they were used for.

BURLEY
[*Startled*]
What did you say?

AUGUSTA
Nothing. The story ended as you said it would.
In a rowdy pack of bitches.

BURLEY
My dear!

AUGUSTA
No sooner opinion out of Burley
Consequence of all his proclamations—

JACK
Free-love—

DUDLEY
Free lunch—

ELISHA
Free everything.

JACK
And naturally the 'Quality' estranged—
46

AUGUSTA

When, naturally, we all took ship at Plymouth.
Came into New York, in late December—

DUDLEY

To a cabin, cocked-up in Pendry Cove—

ELISHA

From Pendry Cove, slap, into Spuyten Duyvil—

AUGUSTA

To a farm, and to an house he called 'Hobbs Ark'.

DUDLEY

A farm he never farmed—

ELISHA

A house he couldn't keep—

AUGUSTA

But to his credit, built the thing himself.

JACK

And not a year standing, when his beasts began to crawl—

AUGUSTA

They do not matter to me now. No more contingent
Than the granite figures up on foreign roofs;
As temperless as tuning-forks unbuzzed.

JACK

[*With a sudden cry*]
Ai-i-i-i-i-i! How they buzzed!

AUGUSTA

[*Sharply*] Who is that fellow?

BURLEY

Why, it was he who found Miranda walking
Down from Dover.

JACK
[*Recovering his composure*] No, Sacré Cœur.


AUGUSTA
Found my daughter walking. Gave her a lift? Well, frankly
I'm not so sure what kind of kindness that was.
What did you say your name sir?


JACK
Jack Blow, Madame.


AUGUSTA
Jack Blow? What sort of name is that?
Come into the light, so. Why do you wear a patch?


JACK
The better to see you with, madame.


AUGUSTA
Levity depraves some part of man—
Mend, boy.


JACK
I mend, madame.


AUGUSTA
Miranda?—Did you say walking?


ELISHA
She's lame.


JACK
Turned her ankle, coming down from church.


AUGUSTA
In some sort of mischief, I've no doubt.


JACK
No madame, war.


AUGUSTA
What!
Dressed as though there were no God—

48

All those feathers blowing from her hat;
And such a drag of velvet!

DUDLEY
                              Stand-in for a final curtain!

AUGUSTA
I didn't know Miranda would be here.

JACK
In the shutting down of Paris, we took off
In whatsoever part we had been playing.

ELISHA
                              Herself, the Duchess!

DUDLEY
Queen of the Night!

ELISHA
Wherein she bit the Devil's thumb.

AUGUSTA
Do not affront her; she's that part of me
I can't afford.

ELISHA
You know we admire her stubbornly,
With prudence!

AUGUSTA
                              Do I?

BURLEY
   [*Changing the subject*]
Did Jeremy have word that you were coming?

AUGUSTA
He said 'Come home to Beewick', gave me no address.
Where then would he be, but here at Burley?

To tell the truth, he's my astonishment.
I wonder, shall I know him when I meet him?
They say he looks like me [*to* BURLEY] I'd say our father.
Guileless, not girlish, disengaged, but taken.


DUDLEY

Think you're going to smell him out?


AUGUSTA

[*Annoyed*]
Your grandfather smelled like hemlock, but he leaned,
Like the hollow weed, close by the wall,
For hearts-ease, and so might Jeremy.


DUDLEY

[*With off-hand impudence*]
'She loved her husband dear-i-lie, but another man twic't as well.'


AUGUSTA

He can do no wrong, if I don't say it.


ELISHA

'When Eve delved, and Adam span—'


AUGUSTA

Forgive them, Jonathan, they're unrecorded.


DUDLEY

He's the image of Papa, in congress gaiters—
Regency Rake.


AUGUSTA

Jeremy is Jeremy.


ELISHA

Which put him to such fright, he bolted,
Twenty years ago.


DUDLEY

She'll have him back—toy monkey on a string.

AUGUSTA

[*To* BURLEY]
I haven't told you how it was with Jeremy,
That is, after reformed from excellence.
He left me, howling in an alien room,
And I can't know why.
Left me stranded on an high bad bed,
With legs too short to tap upon the floor;
Shedding the airy tears of age, and rocking
My one and happy memory, the hour
We went hunting, all alone together,
In the Catskill mountains.

JACK

Hunter, hunting hunter,
Turns the tiger to a rabbit's skin
To wrap his mama Bunting in.

BURLEY

[*Sadly*]
Foxes their holes, birds their nests—but man—

AUGUSTA

The more I see of man, the more bereaved.
When I am gone, Miranda, put me in a tree.
Remember, you who have the habit.

DUDLEY

Hoi, the Queen is dead, long live the Queen!

ELISHA

She's dying tall, she's English!

DUDLEY

When Jeremy was home, it's true we rocked
In his gusts of generosity—
For policy—
But Jeremy once gone, Miranda nothing,
Brother, are we free-beaters!

51

JACK

[*Sarcastically*]

Cent-per-cent?

DUDLEY

Look here, I say stand on your own two feet.
Down with sentiment, and up, by God, with trade!

JACK

The rich enjoyment of cupidity?

AUGUSTA

Oh, be quiet, all of you, or go away.
As I was coming up the terraces of Burley
What should I see? A perishing diameter,
Where once a bandstand stood, and *Kapellmeister* Stack—
Remember Stack?—upon it, like a seal
Pawing the air with consecrated mitten,
In which, like a twig in snow, his baton rocked
Thawing out a trumpet voluntary.

ELISHA

Oom-pa-pa, Umm-pa-pa—I'll bet a go at taps!
[*He snatches up a horn, blowing a passage from Purcell.*]

BURLEY

I give you 'I love, and I must'.

[DUDLEY *beats a drum.*]

AUGUSTA

[*Holding her ears*]
I told you they were talented, or did I?

BURLEY

And once instructed.

AUGUSTA

I was coming to my major-general—

ELISHA

*Your* major-general? Miranda's first cadet.

52

AUGUSTA

[*Ignoring the interruption*]
A very autumn cone he was, all scaled in medals;
Braced in knocking points; ribboned, buckled—
I do love a man who jangles!

ELISHA

[*Wandering about and drawling*]
A-A-a-a-a! 'Froggie would a wooing-go.'

AUGUSTA

Vulgarity!
Jonathan, how do you understand it,
No son of mine has been so favoured
That he died in war?

JACK

In spite of progress, and free-enterprise?

AUGUSTA

                    In spite of everything.

DUDLEY

She mourns as one who could be comforted.

JACK

[*To* AUGUSTA, *in a loud whisper*]
Not so much the bravery is welcome,
As the fortunate removal of the body?

AUGUSTA

[*Startled*]
I trust men till they whisper!

BURLEY

                    Do I remember the major-general?

AUGUSTA

Of course you remember the major-general.

53

Except for the one bold bend that seated him,
Complete upright.

JACK

Cancelled out with great fine sanguine sashes,
Crossing up his guts from hip to hame,
Like a comfit box, *experto crede*.
For epaulettes? A swab of Furies.

ELISHA

[*Turning in from the garden*]
I doubt the whole damned thing—
Conductor Stack *and* the palace medals.

BURLEY

[*Drowsily*]
One two, one two—
Compounded motion, like slow strutting honey,
Polling Thomas Tallis on his hook,
And getting Monteverdi put about.

AUGUSTA

And Couperin.
See how defaulted I am Jonathan.

DUDLEY

See how Miranda's staring at you.

AUGUSTA

O, ho, my foot Miranda!
I think I've hurt my foot.

[MIRANDA *begins to move out*.]

DUDLEY

Why call on Miranda? She's afraid of life.

AUGUSTA

You're a proper fool. She's afraid of nothing.

MIRANDA

Not afraid of life, but your opinion of it.

54

ELISHA

The Ruffian Queen! Miranda's coming out!

AUGUSTA

[*As* MIRANDA *comes toward her*]
My foot, Miranda, I have hurt my foot!

MIRANDA

[*Stooping to her*]

Woman, remember you.

AUGUSTA

Why?

ELISHA

'Chicken today, feathers tomorrow.'

AUGUSTA

Farewell, daughter.

MIRANDA

Hail, Mother.

AUGUSTA

Recall me to them all, Miranda.

DUDLEY

'Make her a child again, just for tonight.'

MIRANDA

The flank-plume of the greater bird of paradise
Racked not more pride, than did the dancing lappet
Prowling at your hip that summer day
When you walked off the world.

AUGUSTA

[*Pensively*]
Your father said: 'Don't wag your bottom!'

BURLEY

That sad, tender and hilarious
Portion of the anatomy—the bottom.

55

AUGUSTA

Jonathan!

ELISHA

But to your mother, though you were Solomon
Is always bare!

BURLEY

You always tease your family?

ELISHA

Sure. I gouge my chin into the shoulder bone,
And whiz my thumb into the buttock joint.

BURLEY
                You do?

ELISHA

I love a leaper.

BURLEY
                The pecking ranks—the jackdaw trick—

DUDLEY

The what?

BURLEY
                He walks behind his love, to kick her down.

AUGUSTA

[*To* BURLEY]
I've bungled my escape.
[*Aloud*]
My sons boisterous, my daughter? Sudden quiet.
When she's quiet—and indeed she's quiet,
As dragging silk upon some unseen chain—
I think it lying—she who is forthright.

DUDLEY

I heard you call her vixen at fifteen.

56

AUGUSTA

She's so ambiguous, that mourning dogs
Follow her off graves, with weeping tongues.
But when she rouses to the mark, I think
She's one of awful virtue, and the Devil.

BURLEY

Am I to assume you happier in sons?

AUGUSTA

Of course, men are a pleasure. What's a woman?

DUDLEY

A cow, sitting on a crumpled grin.

AUGUSTA

Jonathan, pretend they are not here:
You I welcome back to Beewick.

MIRANDA

But he never left.

BURLEY

Staying in one place is man's address—
Mind, I did not say instruction.

AUGUSTA

[*With commendable pride*]
His the hand that shored up Burley:
Nor he would not pull the stops on *vox humana*
As Titus would, no matter how he trembled.

MIRANDA

And Titus trembled, good God, how he trembled!

AUGUSTA

[*Noticing* MIRANDA'S *rings*]
What pretty rings. You never gave me rings.

MIRANDA

[*Giving* AUGUSTA *her rings*]
You never remember any rings I gave you.

57

ELISHA
[*Stepping up to* AUGUSTA, *and tapping her with his closed hand*]
Who killed Cock Robin?

DUDLEY
It's true. She can give the world away
And no one seems to pay the least attention.
Her acts kill themselves, as does the sting the bee.

ELISHA
And what a goad she's got!

AUGUSTA
[*To* MIRANDA]
I'll remember that you held my foot
When I am in my grave.
What do I owe you?

BURLEY
                        Oh, unkind!

ELISHA
There's only one kind inch on any woman—
Between her tot and tail—
There's kindness!

AUGUSTA
[*With shocked and frightened laughter*]
My sons are wonderfully ignoble, Jonathan,
Equality has only made them vulgar;
Forgive them. As for Miranda, brother, tell them
How I was handsomer than she.

BURLEY
I remember you as handsome as my niece,
And both of you as handsome as each other.
You in the winter of your starch
As proud as spring—

AUGUSTA
[*Bridling*]
                        Wasn't I?

BURLEY

A very accordion of pleated linen—

AUGUSTA

Underset in laces, bodkin inched,
Threading a rosy satin 'round the knee.

JACK

Hated the house, and all the housework in it?

AUGUSTA

Impudent!
Miranda, tell them how I must have been
When I was thrown up for the gun.

DUDLEY

Out of nothing I can paint that picture:
Smart ramshackle, as any stable queen.
That stark, strict impeccable askew—

JACK

One associates with rectified disaster—

ELISHA

That standing up, as promised, that full stop—

JACK

                    That variety instructed.

ELISHA

Bodkins?
Papa used 'em, and a cork, swan-upping
Of his drabs, to prove himself promoted
Monarch of the clutch.

AUGUSTA

Don't name his creatures when you speak of me!

ELISHA

Why? You also did exactly what he told you.

59

#### DUDLEY

Uh, held me, an infant, in your arms
While he lashed me with his carriage whip.


#### BURLEY

Is this the thing you hold against your father?


#### DUDLEY

I have against my father that he whipped me
*Before I knew him.*


#### MIRANDA

That's what puzzles children—


#### ELISHA

*And* that mother, dutiful and balking
Lived cheek-by-jowl with all his brats and brides;
Slaved, without undue astonishment,
The while the ladies lapped up cakes and ale.


#### DUDLEY

Come down! The biddies drank their coffee black.
All in the selfsame sty, except of course Augusta
Down on her knees, with holy-stone and soap
Scrubbing 'round grandmother, missionary,
Knitting 'little things' for the Swahili.


#### ELISHA

                Oh, come again.


#### DUDLEY

Father, marking in the book of Genesis:
'Give me my wives and children, for whom I have served thee, and
    let me go.'
Hypocrite and Emperor. Sufficient
To a thousand geese, like Abraham.


#### AUGUSTA

    [*Starting from her chair, which sends her sons backing away*]
Oh, madness to know anyone!

ELISHA

[*Ducking, but continuing the banter*]
All the while that mule, Brigid-Matilda
(His first paramour, popped out of placket)
Stitched on her hoop of bloody twist,
Crying in a loud voice, to her needle:
'We'll sew us out of bondage yet!'

BURLEY

                    Did she?

AUGUSTA

[*Sitting down again*]
That I should be reminded now and here
Of all the gaudy that has gone before.
    [*To* BURLEY]
She was *not* the one who got away.
Where do we sleep tonight?

BURLEY

                    It is arranged.

AUGUSTA

Good. Then let us speak of Beewick as our country.

DUDLEY

Don't mind us. We're only poor provincials.

AUGUSTA

Off with you! I'm talking to my brother
Of the time when you were not at all.
Jonathan was Norman, I not tame—

ELISHA

[*Braying*]

                    Hee-haw, Hee-haw!

AUGUSTA

My brindled tweed full gallooned to the foot,
With hems that haunted everywhere I walked;
While about my head a leghorn reeled
Bridling in the wind.

DUDLEY

[*Pretending admiration*]
No!

ELISHA

[*Taking him up*]
Yes. A daring act of caution, cut to size.
Hips as chaste as slate to tailor to—

AUGUSTA

Play the fool, patronize yourself.

DUDLEY

The coif seized upward on a murd'rous pin
Till the bared bone, under shaking mull
Reared up an ear, like to a crescent fluke
To stay the browsing fall—

AUGUSTA

Whose browse?

ELISHA

Why father's—what else?

DUDLEY

Old Baron Ox.

ELISHA

The whole thing sounds, I'd say, more like Miranda.

AUGUSTA

Let it be Miranda.
Miranda's all Augusta laid up in Miranda;
Born again to be my new account—
And all my candidature.
Daughter, when I die, I charge you, lay me in a tree,
I'll hop to heaven.

DUDLEY

Back in trees again!

ELISHA

When the bough bends?

#### DUDLEY
What is Miranda profits your estate?

#### ELISHA
What profit anyone who trips the foreign scene?

#### DUDLEY
And prefers her bloodshed in an alien tongue
And is said to write her comedies in French.
As far as I am concerned, expatriate's
The same as traitor.

#### BURLEY
        Then my son, you are in darkness.

#### DUDLEY
Don't misunderstand me, we all loved the lamb—
Till she turned mutton.

#### AUGUSTA
If one child was to be a gifted child
It should have been a boy, and that boy Jeremy.
But Titus overwhelmed all but Miranda.
You do remember my dead husband, Jonathan?

#### BURLEY
Alas my dear, and all that way from London.

#### AUGUSTA
        Hearing you a master of the organ—

#### JACK
Came to learn, stayed to instruct?

#### BURLEY
        And with him his mother.

#### AUGUSTA
If there's to be description of Victoria
I'll give her.

63

JACK

Middletown Récamier no doubt.

AUGUSTA

The absolute rage of London.
All the grandees of the day pulled at her door,
Just like cranes at feeding time. The artists,
The most eccentric, and the most renowned.
Just for a cat-nip, and but late of Hang-town
Lotta Crabtree sang upon her lap,
As it had been a last command performance.

JACK

Making England safe for London?

DUDLEY

[*Snappishly*]
What do you know about it!

MIRANDA

Free-soiler, free-thinker, nonconformist.
Abolitionist, Hyde Park orator—

AUGUSTA

But kept the Benedictine in the caddy!

JACK

Titus, with the broad parochial stare,
Of a Sankey and a Moody ranter;
Ravished by the knocking sisters Fox,
Done in by snobbery and levitations;
Watching mandolines lay hands upon their stresses
Sailing 'round the rafters of the room.

ELISHA

And ended up a silly spry old fool
High hat and all!

DUDLEY

Old ladies do adore a frisky party!

64

#### AUGUSTA
[*Again rising, in indignation*]
If there's one thing less pleasing than another,
It's a brisk and nimble antic man,
Who, to prove himself both young and able,
Leaps over hedge and ditch, clashing his castors.
I am a grave and proper woman.

#### DUDLEY
Proper!
You've pissed like a cat to hear of lechery!

#### AUGUSTA
[*Sitting down again*] O!

#### ELISHA
[*Aside to* DUDLEY]
That's torn it!

#### DUDLEY
[*Aside to* ELISHA]
Patience. Keep it fast, keep it funny.

#### AUGUSTA
I wonder who we are, we still have time for it.
I who loved all things fastidious
Get me lewd men.

#### DUDLEY
What else? We're timely.

#### AUGUSTA
And without innocence;
Nor have you the special dispensation of Daguerre,
Whose any touch was new baptism laid.
Beneath his stroke your father was a child.
His love-locks then did fret his cheeks as youth
Had found new courtesy.

#### JACK
But his chin un-saw'd like mine?

AUGUSTA

Who are you, young man, to know
How a widow's dead man looks?

JACK

Checkmate!

AUGUSTA

On his cheek-bones' plush, bees buzzed and hung
As he had been a park.

MIRANDA

I thought you said you never liked the man.

AUGUSTA

Except his teeth. His teeth were my delight.

MIRANDA

Defend a better point; four children hang upon it.

AUGUSTA

None of you were anywhere when I first saw him.

BURLEY

A man who crept around his own circumference.
As he were looking for the exit.
    [*To the sons*]
How do you see your father?

JACK

    [*Off guard*]
That old Ram! Cock-pit Bully Boy!

AUGUSTA

Our coachman is an orator!

JACK

[*Bowing*] At your service, madam.

DUDLEY

Fe-fo-fi-fum—I smell the blood of an Englishman!

#### AUGUSTA

[*Paying no attention*]
He was of the self-appointed race American.

#### BURLEY

In our hey-day many came to Burley,
Your father was but one among the hurly.
Apologists and special pleaders came,
Peers, encyclopaedists, architects—
They said they came to chart our bull-nosed beams—
And not one but somehow lost his balance
And all but toppled headlong for his brougham
Ogling my shy and cunning sisters—
The little peeking brigantines!

#### AUGUSTA

Barristers and watchful judges came
Balancing their verdict on their knee—
That second outward ponder of the head—
The curled, full-bottomed wig of jurisprudence.

#### BURLEY

Gentle folk, who proved to be unkind;
Chaplains, jobbers, and processions came:
Once, and only once, with wild prophetic eye
The dean.

#### MIRANDA

And Victoria?

#### AUGUSTA

I said if it's to be Victoria, I'll give her.
There was one who thought herself of Royal Jelly,
And had, she said, the touch was once the King's.
Was I, a country girl, to disbelieve her?
May I be forgiven, I believed her utterly;
She was so tender and perfidious;
A faulty scholar, but a witty one:
And such a pair of transcendental eyes!

#### BURLEY

Late out of Bangkok, for the press.

## AUGUSTA

When having run her ways, backed into dock,
(Her more than Oriental rooms in Grosvenor Square);
An awesome hull in feral brilliants paved,
Wearing on her head a turban's bale,
A coil twice as cunning as her mind—
Her draw-glove thrown in among the Lions
(The choicest of her guests rolled in the swell!)—
Followed by a Blackamoor and spaniel
The spaniel followed by her second husband,
All ivory tush, and fearful waxed moustaches,
A Spaniard of the utmost rich vulgarity
Whom, for much love, she'd married with two rings—
(He left her later for a Cheapside Strumpet)—
Well, be that as it may—*Enter Victoria!*

## JACK

In such bight and squall of twinklings shod,
Her tasselled, taped and parried abdomen,
Banded like the skin-trussed boxer-hornet,
Hummed and shook beneath the midnight lamps:
And at its middle swung the drowsy stone
Named for the moon.

## DUDLEY

[*Crowing with admiration*] Cock-a-doodle-do!

## AUGUSTA

Though not proper that you marry twice,
And certainly improper to have lovers,
(In her mind all love was truth and honour—
She was mourned indeed by fifty silk umbrellas—
It always rains straight down on prodigies)
She could cluck in anyone for daughter.
She whistled and the girls, like thieves, came running;
A ready and a milking tongue could stroke
One out of store as quick as any ant
As keeps a cow.

## ELISHA

'Mademoiselle was new at court, and nervous!'

'And had but a penny a day'—

AUGUSTA

She had my purse, my person, and my trust
In one scant hour.
Even stones wear down beneath the lick of flattery
And I but rock-salt to her stallion son,
Before whose rough unbridled head I dwined
At his fast leisure.

BURLEY

Poor, wretched and unhappy child!

AUGUSTA

He became so sure of his sufficience,
Blew his own horn; composed his own libretti—
Sawed the gryphon up, the what-not down;
Voiced the whooping clocks to keep his hours;
Wrote his own credo, kept his own accounts,
And, maul-stick *en garde*, and palette at careen,
Painted the company a brick-house red.

JACK

But, to slake a thirst more raging than Narcissus
Leaning at the brink, the cod fell in.

DUDLEY

He had a way of rising on rebuke.

ELISHA

And vain! A child's block underneath his heel
And he was up and crowing like a cock.

AUGUSTA

What a tandem that was!
I've had it on the best authority
Vesta Victoria sang in Leicester Square
'Behold the ears of my heart are set before thee',
Just to please Victoria, that old woman!

Rake, God knows, footpad and Regent bawd;
As mad a peddler's kingdom as conceivable.


MIRANDA

But in the dead of winter, rode a Gothic sleigh
To fetch the bacon home.

AUGUSTA

                         Scavenger.

MIRANDA

   [*Controlling her anger*]
Do not frequent her absence. There was one
Knew how to be a scavenger.
Her rip-tide bore up and rocked our cradle.
Ship-chandler she, to any wreck off coast.
A creeping shrine, keel barnacled, and listing
Under the children's votive offerings,
Marbles, ribbons, pebbles, broken dolls
And all such things that frightened children leave
In tigers' dens. A staggered sanctuary
With a circus and a juggler on her back:
She knew how to frighten totally.
Peddler, puddler, foot-pad, lean-to, grot;
Of Hogarth kind, of Goya time, Forain—
But as St. Peter shut the door, her heel
Stayed by, to let the children through.


AUGUSTA

You always took her side.

MIRANDA

                         Did I?

AUGUSTA

But I, poking finger in my counterpane
Felt what? A woman caterpillar to my touch,
And knew her son Bull Titus had commenced
The monstrous practice of polygamy.


DUDLEY

In short—beast one.

70

AUGUSTA
                    Exactly.


BURLEY
My dear sister, why were you surprised?
Titus began his practice here in Beewick.
How far he went, no one this age can say:
He flushed one siren, certainly, pecking a zither
Under the mustard's foot.


JACK
Miss Mephistopheles!


BURLEY
    [*Faintly amused*]
Wolfed in cardinal even to galoshes
All in scarlet, as the checker, berry skin;
A cherry ribbon 'round her neck, as murdered.
Once on the stairs, she mounted like a lizard
Crying 'Are you intense?'


DUDLEY
    [*Who has got himself up in the gallery*]
Was that Louise, with the butt librarian;
You know—looking for a good book, on low shelf?


ELISHA
It was not. It was the trollop bawled
'Sic' 'em!' to the visions in her mind—
The one that dad hooked off a barge in Erie.


AUGUSTA
No, no. You're mixing that one with Belinda.
Belinda was, thank God, before your time.
You refer to Juliette of Camberwell.


DUDLEY
Have we got fun!
I was thinking of Kitty Partingale,
The one grandmother hauled in Blackpool,
Or was it Brighton? Anyway a harper
Harping on her harp in cockle time.

71

JACK

Plucking its high-hipped shrouds, with insect teasings.
It's said she got no further than 'The Little Nipper'
When your grandmother snared her.

AUGUSTA

[*Tartly*]
She was playing Mozart, and it was Covent Garden.

DUDLEY

Whichever lay it was, knocked down for tone.

AUGUSTA

[*In a loud whisper to* BURLEY, *who is nodding*]
Don't move, and do not go to sleep!
[*Aloud*]
Kitty was the silliest of them all.

MIRANDA

A lost clairvoyant, that is all, poor creature.
Said she saw Lord Kitchener in a cloud
Chasing Oom Paul Kreuger over Africa,
Waving the Doomsday Book before him as he ran.

AUGUSTA

[*Suddenly snapping her fingures*] Trudy Frisch from Bruges!
There was an estimable vixen cleared his bed;
One Fleming who, in pride of grease
Kept it for her countrymen.

JACK

'In tender grass sat Phyllis' fighting
Tooled in beauty anyway she turned.

MIRANDA

No matter how she rolled, the raging sun
Fleeced her verge with bright and shining mane;
And where the wrestle lashed among the rushes
Up came Jeremy, that bullish baby, clapping
His left hind thumb-wing in his father's face,
Lisping 'Seducer!'

72

BURLEY

Out of the frying-pan, into the fire.

DUDLEY

You said it.
When the law caught up with us, behind the wall—
Which he'd built up high for fear of tongues—
He burned his credo, chucked up his account.
Thus having utterly betrayed betrayal
Turned us out like bastards, being none:
Hauled off on a stone-boat from the Cove
That he might make at least one hussy legal.

BURLEY

And then he died?

AUGUSTA

He dawdled more than died.

BURLEY

I never really understood how you condoned it.

AUGUSTA

Don't come at me too! I was a victim:
I've done my duty to the state—in children.

ELISHA

Oh, not *that* again.

AUGUSTA

He claimed himself a Saint of such a Latter day
Would sweep the world of whores; I but believed him.

BURLEY

My dear girl!

AUGUSTA

In my day we did not leave our husbands.

JACK

Particularly when he put on side
Pretending to the Earldom of old Pendry?

73

ELISHA

O heavens, and the Baron of Castaigne!
For sheer impudence and foreign tone
Went scratching in the barnyard straw
Searching his escutcheon.


DUDLEY

Spitting prunes among the Philistines;
A Puritan too close to his apostasy,
And of such tender sensibility
Burned mother's feather boa, but killed the cocks.


BURLEY

I was afraid of it. But you Augusta,
Though balancing a kingdom in your mind,
How did you lose the purpose of your life?
Our squires of Burley
Had no need of prophets in the midst
To ask them on which side it was they dressed,
They bred their state upon them as they went,
Dressed fitly, as the velvet to the horn.
In fortitude they were all over Burley;
In whatsoever key they tolled, they belled
Forthright, even to the cannon. So I find
It more than strange that you wore Titus.


AUGUSTA

He said he was the stud to breed a kingdom.


JACK

[*Humming*]
'Who passes by this road so late'—
Look: a pedigree's not got by rubbing, lady
Two nights together.


BURLEY

[*Rising in haste*] I'll fetch the lamps.


DUDLEY AND ELISHA

Take Jack with you.

AUGUSTA

[*Holding* BURLEY] Don't move.
[*Aloud*]
Of course, there's always snaffle in opinion.
Say I was sitting on an ottoman
Swallowing, in a gulp, the Trinity—
Father, son and unholy cause.


JACK

That was the day the sky fell down on chicken—


AUGUSTA

That was the day that story-book Augusta
Feather-headed, fairy-tale Augusta
In her mind's wild latitude laid out
And armed such battlefield, tilt patch and list
As out-geared Mars. My maximed mind
Out-maximed circus Maximus.
I hung the bright shields up, I spun the drill,
Clubbed the spears and standards, axe and mace.
I teased the olive, and all budding things
Into the loop that wheels a victor's head
And for his blood their own bright berries drop.
I snared the empty target of the heart—
That builds its nest in metal chains and rings—
With the colours of a ghosted mother:
Planted the visored helmet, shark-side up
And to its yawn I threw my gauntlet in.
Then, then I waited for the clash of arms.
And what did my sons? Did rise and prime
Along the march, like Burnam Wood?
No. Lay by, and fiddled!
*Moles* could have trooped it!


BURLEY
                              Miranda did.


AUGUSTA

Who's Miranda?
She gives her weapons to the enemy.

75

Look how in magnificence defeated!
In short, I can't afford her
She's only me.

BURLEY

You, but only more offended.

AUGUSTA
Well, well, enough of that; I'm starving.

BURLEY

Then here's where Jack comes in.
He tells me he has a catch of Burley treasures
Should strip the town of bread.
Jump Jack! Go fetch my sister supper.

JACK

[*Starting off*]
Count me gone no longer than your blessing.

[*Exit*]

AUGUSTA
A wild and saucy air.

BURLEY

A wild and saucy fellow. I would say
Fond of Miranda, for her style.
And puzzled.

AUGUSTA

If you ask me—and no one ever asks me—
I'd say Miranda's in the ink-fish fog
Thrown off by her father, when recanting
Now many years ago. She has indeed the air
Ruthless as the damned in heaven;
Yet in abandon of variety
She's lost the journey of her life
As does the owl the journey of his head.

BURLEY

In short, you are mistaken.

76

AUGUSTA

In short you seem to think so; still it's known
She's been in and out of wills, like dogs through hoops.
Somehow, some way, my children *must* be marvellous.

ELISHA

[*Cracking nuts*] Why?
Who are you to rate a marvellous child.
As for Miranda, she was always wrapped
In such confounded condescending clemency
I wouldn't trust her, even were she slapped.

DUDLEY

Mother always liked her when her head was hanging.

AUGUSTA

When a little girl, the look was charming—

DUDLEY

You had her so convinced she was the devil,
At seven she was cutting down the hedges
To furnish brier to beat her to your favour,
Then went out hunting for the crime.

ELISHA

Wait now, that reminds me of that dog
That mongrel that you held down with both hands,
At father's orders, while he aimed and cored it
With a blunderbus, rammed down with your love-letters.

BURLEY

A wicked thing a child should see the moon
Rise in the belly of a dog.
Didn't *anybody* get away?

AUGUSTA

Flora, the nameless one.
He laid that girl housekeeping in the earth.
Greenland got her, doubled down and cozy
To her brat.

77

#### MIRANDA

I sometimes wonder what it is a woman
Sweats between her palms when she's being merciful.

#### AUGUSTA

Don't look at me! Your father was to blame
For everything.

#### MIRANDA

Yes he was. Yet was he not the man
Lay thrashing on the floor, one kill night through?
Death's first deposit, his dead bastard child,
Face shut, foreclosed, and in its golden burr
Riding the saddle of his pounding heart,
Where he struck foot, as running up the air
To fail her exit, clapping hands and shouting
'Halt!' There was a cry.

#### ELISHA

Still mother wept the strings, and still she craked
'Cuckoo'.

#### MIRANDA

And still dung-beetle Atlas carries on.

#### BURLEY

Still I do believe Elvire started it—
Our sister; a girl who stroked the heart but breathing.
But to name her as the world would name her—lurcher—
It was her foot tripped our Lord Dearly down.
Yet, of such phlegm, she let him palm her off
To a chap in busby.

#### AUGUSTA

A busby that he groomed just like a cat.

#### BURLEY

The very back-sides of his buttons whistled!

#### AUGUSTA

[*Stubbornly*] It was Victoria.

Titus?

AUGUSTA
The two between them could so gild a mischief,
Though it festered to high heaven, smelled most sweet.


DUDLEY
Posh! Tossed his biddies headlong in the ring,
Upon whose fighting heels, may it be noted,
According who the pullet for the day,
Slashed his wicked spurs.


AUGUSTA
I still hear the distant whining of his gulls
Down the furthest reaches of my ear:
Procuress, procured, and bastard!


MIRANDA
*Et cetera, et cetera, et cetera!*
If you, who were once docile, ardent, credent
Can say that to us now, then I say, madame,
You are in husband, child and every act
A most abominable cheat.


AUGUSTA
I say sluts!
Pander, beast, and prostitutes!


MIRANDA
Hear me:
And if you hear, when you hear
The infinitely distant, pining voice
Of any creature punished in the web,
Or spinning sorrows trap-door in your ear,
Or, broken on the wheel of bitter vision
Some phantom shatter on the glacier of your eye,
Some spirit buzz the shutter of your heart:
If the unleashed hand of Cicero, your hand
Spreads to his creeping octave, on your wall,
And having writ '*non nobis*' in your script

Moves on, then under the listing of the Veil
Either other's head, empalmed, incline.
Find her, if you find her, turn her:
Stroke out misfortune's fortune.

AUGUSTA

Oh my God!
To everybody I'm the other person!

BURLEY

[*Quickly, to* MIRANDA]
Come, niece, help me with the lamps.

[*Exeunt* BURLEY *and* MIRANDA]

AUGUSTA

[*Nervous on finding herself alone with her sons*]
I wonder what it is Miranda's dressed for.
Though compounded of a thousand ills,
Embroidered, and embossed for some high scandal,
She is, all in all, magnanimous—

ELISHA

So? The whole fool's present in Miranda.

DUDLEY

If rigged for anything it's trouble.
A strolling player indeed! Without Protector,
Husband, son or bank-account? Phizz, phizz!
She'd better been a strolling salesman,
With all that *tutti* and *continuo*;
And walking 'round creation once a day,
And been no menace to our purse.

AUGUSTA

Don't falsify. She never whined your purses.
What I find strange is that she is not famous.
I really thought she'd get into the papers.
She's met everyone of any consequence.
Would she make a note of their addresses?
No, she would not.

80

ELISHA

Still you swept the strings, and still she cried
'My mother, oh my mother!'


AUGUSTA

I've observed the more my daughter lives
Up to the general precepts of her scruples
The more she is abandoned.


ELISHA

She's resented according how she rates:
Those who can't afford her, push her.


AUGUSTA

Who pushed her?


DUDLEY

You pushed her.


ELISHA

When you, grass-widow, were set out to pasture,
Finding it a time of locusts and of famine—
Thinking only of your sons—and rightly so—
Pushed her, into the dark, as sole provider,
And she as green as any simpleton—


AUGUSTA

[*Trembling*]
Don't you dare that speech before my brother!
Miranda didn't need a push, she went.
Are you so derelict of common custom
You bait your mother to her consternation?
Then I do not hear you.


DUDLEY

[*Grinning*]
Deaf, sure; but break wind in a muff
Then do you startle.


ELISHA

And when she startles with her carving knife—
Three boy mice, see how they run!

AUGUSTA

[*In a level, telling voice*]
You'd not lose so much as one *castrato*
His dear weight; not hang you in the voice
To bruit my tale, nor any grief in alt;
Nor you never bought *me* anything to flaunt!

DUDLEY

[*As always, when she is sharp, more pleased than offended*]
                              Gad! Spirit—what!

[*At this moment* JACK *enters with a mutton bone and mug. He presents them to* AUGUSTA *with a flourish. She accepts with a child's thoughtless gusto.*]

JACK

Allow me, madame, as good Sir Thomas said:
'All flesh that we behold'—you know—'in at the mouth'—
Remember it.
    [*Making for the door*]
If you'll excuse me, I'm knocking up high-tea,
In the pantry.

AUGUSTA

[*Her mouth full*]
Hear anything of Jeremy?

JACK

                    Jeremy? Not a word of Jeremy.

[BURLEY *and* MIRANDA *enter, with lamps.*]

AUGUSTA

[*Regarding the mutton bone*]
Truly, a monstrous munching earth. But stand upon it
And you find you stand on appetite.
Age? A tenant fool—all fork and pot,
And unpremeditated sleep.

DUDLEY

I say reign, for God's sake, or get off the pot!

82

#### BURLEY
[*Setting his lamp under the shadow of the balcony*]
No light may show.

#### MIRANDA
[*Setting her lamp under the wing of the lay figure*]
Starlight would have seen us through.

#### JACK
Bless you, *and* darkness, I'm off.

[*Exit*]

#### AUGUSTA
[*Noticing for the first time the vines that have encroached on the hall*]
See how the bind-weed hauls against the ground
And on the winch of autumn puts out hooks,
To clamber greatness down. How like the vine,
The female-vetch, that low perfidious crawl,
That winding thief with estuary mouth
That nibbles at the root, and topples boys,
And thinks by climbing to the privet of the head
To be the glory that she fattens on.

#### ELISHA
[*Whistling*]

Couldn't be anyone we know?

#### DUDLEY
Nor anybody standing in this hall?

#### AUGUSTA
Why not, dear Dudley?

#### DUDLEY
Because, damn it, we're neither crowned nor credited—
Which is, I will admit, a monstrous blunder.

#### ELISHA
Though handsomely well-heeled, I'm sure my wife
Married me for money, lovely money.

Exactly and that is decline.
Glory used to be the thing—now it's possessions.
My heart's as heavy as the emery
I stick my needles in to say it.
But I know women, son. Before I'm cold
They'll have me off the sheets, as I were fag
And thrown up in the air to my new office.
Before you can say 'Knife!' take pot and pan;
Snatch my very pediment; and from my poke,
(With finger-tips like greedy Florentines
Compounding pledge against the 'Haemorrhage of time')
Take all, clasping my hand, for sorrow's sign.
Though in truth but cunning's gyve, to grapple
The finger-rings from hungry *rigor mortis*.
Then will they ease.

DUDLEY
[*Leaning forward, hands on knees*]
Son-of-a-sea-cook, is she tender!

MIRANDA
And correct.

AUGUSTA
I've seen the creatures when they thought
My third eyelid was down.

ELISHA
How is it that some women have no breasts
Till they have buried children?

AUGUSTA
[*Starting straight up, then sitting down again*]
Oh, unnatural, brutish villain! You nursed me standing;
The suckle-canker yet hangs on your lip!
[DUDLEY *claps his hands.*]

BURLEY
If I might put in a word—

AUGUSTA

Words, words! I would that I'd been shrew,
I'd have pegged my bosom to a thorn:
Or that I'd been the convoy-fish whose maw
Is swamp and cradle to its spawn—
I'd have rocked my children up!

MIRANDA

[*Hotly, to her brothers*]
Base, base!
The fearful purpose of the tiger's prowl,
Consulted in that inch the paw debates,
Was not more still than mine,
When from our mother's stalk I cut you down
And held you like a turtle on my hand—
Saint and turtle are the same upon their backs—
And wondered, then, which of the two I'd caught.

ELISHA

[*Making the sound of shivering*]
*Brrrrr!* The climate of the hand was cold.

MIRANDA

The climate of the hand was terror. Taking purpose
For ferocity is how you lose me.

AUGUSTA

You all seem to know much more than I do.
I, like the poor man-handled mendicant
Sit down alone, to banquet in a dream;
Say I mothered children in a vision.

BURLEY

[*Sadly*]
Has any here, against a worser day
Laid by one kinsman in his sentry-box
To patrol the after time? Not one?
Nothing for the winter of estrangement?

DUDLEY
[*With derision*] Sure, Miranda.

85

BURLEY

Though I met Miranda much too late
I've found her, in most part, full excellent.

DUDLEY

Why sure, but there's depopulation in her yaw.

BURLEY

Augusta, how do you find?

AUGUSTA

In this last, worst hour of my astonishment
I find that I'm a fool.
I've walked me in the Strand and Piccadilly;
I've stroken the lions in Trafalgar Square,
I learned everything in Pendry Cove, yet still
I don't improve, because I won't ask questions.
I won't ask questions because I find I sweat me
In three several horrid generations,
And would know nothing.

JACK

[*Entering*]
The damned, who won't capitulate!
    [*To* BURLEY, *who is nodding*]
Hi, warden! Wake up! We're off.

BURLEY

[*Starting*] Eh? What?

JACK

Give me a hand. I've got a thing in boot
Is timely.

[*Exeunt* BURLEY *and* JACK. *They are no sooner gone than silently and swiftly the two sons*—DUDLEY *donning a pig's mask*, ELISHA *an ass's, as if the playthings would make them anonymous*—*rush the two women.* ELISHA *knocks* MIRANDA'S *cane away, seizing her and pinning her arms behind her.* DUDLEY *pushing* AUGUSTA *about in an attempt to make her dance.*]

DUDLEY

I'll huff, and I'll puff, and I'll blow your house down!

AUGUSTA
[*Thinking they are really playing*]
A tilt!


DUDLEY
[*Dropping her, dancing about in a crouching position, striking out in
light rapid taps, as of a boxer sparring*]
Want to play with baby? Going to play with baby?
Who's afraid?
He'll let you off at Windsor.


ELISHA
[*Pushing* MIRANDA *from behind with his knee, still holding her
arms*]
Now then, my somewhat well-used spinster,
Now that your precious uncle Jonathan
Has for the moment turned down his metronome
And bushel'd off, what shan't we do with you?
You'd never listen to your brothers, would you, Toots?
Tick-bird, riding out the Grand Conception,
Which father, for lack of guts, left in your corner.
    [*Raising his knee*]
Let us see, if by your scumber, you are fox!


DUDLEY
[*Over his mother's shoulder, to* ELISHA]
Slap her ears down. Stand her on four feet!
That'll set her up! I'd say that's one position
Of which she hasn't made the most in twenty years.


ELISHA
The damned and dedicated 'victim'. Just another
Self-appointed increment! I never knew
Such an earnest stinker!
Why couldn't you live up to your brothers?


AUGUSTA
[*Out of breath, to* MIRANDA]
You never would—you know you never would
Listen to your brothers.

MIRANDA

[*Suddenly freeing herself*]
Hands off, you too near thing!
[*To* AUGUSTA]
Would you that I leap into myself
There dismiss me of my occupation
To set me in the slum of their regard?
Would have me clapped between the palms of their approval?
Get me rated
In the general horror of the common mouth;
And to the verdict of the vulgar, stand me down
Crying 'I'm a fool!' to ease a fool?


DUDLEY

Snap her ears: crack her crown with thimbles.
Look out, boys, the dam has bust!


MIRANDA

There is a kind of ticking in a little man
Announces him his uninvited soul.


ELISHA

[*Kicking* MIRANDA'S *skirt*]
That amulet you wore upon your leg—
Not rusted yet?

> [*Loud laughter.* DUDLEY, *now in possession of* JACK'S *whip, makes darting motions with it at* AUGUSTA. *His and* ELISHA'S *remarks follow so closely they are spoken in a sort of free-for-all.*]


DUDLEY

[*To* AUGUSTA]
Hi! I love to see a sway-back on the run;
It's game to haul a bang-tail by the scut;
It's rare to watch a crab stuck on a skewer
When the parasite is sidling in for keeps!


ELISHA

[*To* MIRANDA]
Ho! continental shoat—eh? Got the staggers?
Made the run from gate-post to the gate?

88

Got best rating from the bloody intellectuals?
Aristocrat, pauper, artist, beggar!
[*Snapping his fingers over her head, as in show*]
Trim, trim, up, up! Quarter—quarter!
Who's going to run again, wayfarer stalking
In the earth? Not you, not ever you.
Toss-pot, salamander, rake-hell, punk!
You'll be crawling in my gutters yet
If I don't watch it—with your starving puss
Like some abominable slug of vengeance, risen
Waist-high, pointing your shaking finger at me.
And who can stand a beggar who can point
Even in her most 'distinguished' drunkenness?
Get yourself an occupation—souser!


### MIRANDA

If drink for drink, mine, business strategy, as yours:
If for my brother Brutus I belched dollars,
I'd find he wore me to the elbow.
Merchant—away with you!


### ELISHA

Away with you, says she!
Do you think by your rank continence to stay
The generations?
[*Seizing her*]
Manless, childless, safeless document—
I'll staff you!

[*He is weeping as he mauls her.*]


### MIRANDA

[*Quietly pushing him away*]
Do not think to climb me, brother.
See how it is with man who has no history
To make him innocent. See how deaf the face is.
How the crouching tongue turns in the mouth
To sting me down; look how pricks up his ear!
You'll rump it to the judgement seat, poor trader,
Dragging the lumber of your tail.

ELISHA

[*Standing back*]
Damnation and the devil!
[*He trips her*]

Sanded, am I?

Then go be my wag!


DUDLEY

Look, the mendicant bell-wether's down.
Who's sanded now!


AUGUSTA

Let her go.
Should she drop the flag of her surrender,
Do not pick it up: it charges in the cambric.


ELISHA

[*Giving* MIRANDA *a violent shove towards* AUGUSTA]
She's your hound; do as you like with her.


AUGUSTA

[*Considering the recommendation*]
Even dogs are not abandoned in a ruin, Elisha.


ELISHA

Oh yes, they are. It's practice keeps them fast,
And what other practice has she than her ruin?
If we take her home and loose her on our ledgers,
She'll blot us up.


AUGUSTA

Fie, fie! I've seen my daughter die before, and make it.


DUDLEY

[*Swinging* JACK'S *whip before him*]
The sun being in the lower ward, you plead her?
[*He turns the whip, handle down, making imaginary squares on the
ground, as children do in street games*]
'Step upon a crack, you break your mother's back—'
Why then, jump, old woman, jump! jump off the world!
Be dead, be done, be modest dead, be quick!

90

A snipe can smell his meat ten inches underground;
On scent, old crow, downward to the feast!
[*He attempts to make her dance,* AUGUSTA *tries to obey, her mouth open as one who screams*]
Dance! Dance! Dance!

AUGUSTA
Eighty's a cold mouse!

DUDLEY
[*Whirling her about*] Who's eighty yet?

MIRANDA
[*Coming between them*]
Stop it!
[*To* AUGUSTA]
Unclench the cramp in Dudley's hand, poor woman.
As some rudiment of forgotten nature squalls
In the horned-toad's eye, that it spills blood
Who is too hideous to mourn, so your son's palm
Might yet spill his lost innocence in kind,
The baby fleece he cropped, up journeying his crib.
There is he mapped—if he be mapped at all—
Yet I think, that of himself, he's washed his either hand.

[BURLEY *and* JACK *enter, carrying a covered object. Placing it in the centre of the table,* JACK *pulls the cover off, exposing a doll's house.* DUDLEY *and* ELISHA *hurriedly unmask, holding the masks underarm.*]

JACK
[*Quietly*]
I give you Hobb's Ark, beast-box, doll's house—
That little alchemy unhems a man.
Madame, your contagion.

ELISHA
Here's The House That Jack Built:
Feed her to the toy!

[*He lifts* AUGUSTA *to the table, unprotesting. Cross-legged she sits before the toy, picking up the first thing to catch her attention—a stick hung with dolls.*]

91

AUGUSTA

Tumblers! Seven straightened mistresses!
   [*She pushes the lock on the roof of the doll's house, and up pops a
   doll*]
Why, it's your father, Titus, tamed! An imp,
A midge, a tick, a peg, a bob, a gnat,
A syllable all buttoned up in cypress!
A chip, a doll, a toy, a pawn,
A little man soon cooled. A nothing!
Now he has struck a size that suits him!
Was this the stick that leapt me, gentlemen?
Where now the stallion yard lay beating on the turf
Its whistling vent? So proud of it he was
He asked to be but laid beside it in the grave.


JACK
                    Tall burial?


ELISHA

Watch her go!


AUGUSTA

This size I could have jumped him
And been happily unacquainted with you all.
   [*Scanning the puppet*]
A thieving magpie's borne his beard away!


MIRANDA

To build a nest on Babylon.


JACK

Evoe! You have an husband in the hand,
A slave, a fit of pine to do your bidding.
Was this the inch that set you out at hack?
Then 'tis a kissing splinter for a catch,
And you can game again.


MIRANDA
   [*Sharply*]
On what errand was the knife that sharpened this?

92

JACK

Wood-offering.

AUGUSTA

Whose malice was it hacked him down?

JACK

Mine.

AUGUSTA

I said, who are you that you should know
How a widow's dead man looks?

JACK

Nobody, madame.

AUGUSTA

Miranda's been talking.

JACK

Possibly.

AUGUSTA

Not any theme at all will make this strut again.

MIRANDA

Now has the mountain fallen on Mohammed.

AUGUSTA

How do we thaw from history. How many
To this splinter have made careful love
Like porcupines. What apes our eyes are
Saw him great because he said so.
So, lay him down.

MIRANDA

If death's a green unruly thumb, I'd say
Do not lay down that breeding inch; it was the cause.

JACK

[*Tapping on the attic window of the doll's house*]
Put your wink against this window pane, what do you see?

93

AUGUSTA

[*Putting her eye to the small window*]
A bedroom, no bigger than my hand.


MIRANDA

Do you remember what that cock-loft saw?
For that window is become your eye.
What do you see?


AUGUSTA

[*Recoiling*]
I don't care what you've done, I do forgive me.


MIRANDA

*Do* you?


AUGUSTA

[*With great agitation*]
Stop it, Miranda. I'm a stranger here.


JACK

Stranger, or accomplice?


AUGUSTA

I do not understand you.


JACK

No? Look to.


AUGUSTA

[*Her chin on the window ledge*]
As in a glass darkly, a frost of fury spent—
As ghosts of hot-house plants in summer shed
A static flight impaled upon the pane:
As in a profaned monstrance, see conspire
The fighting shadow of the Devil and the Daughter.


JACK

The girl, damned, with her instep up-side-down,
Dragging rape-blood behind her, like the snail.
Whimpering 'Glory, glory!'

94

#### MIRANDA

Howling 'Glory, Glory!' for the god
In the cinders of that blasphemy.
And beneath her, in a lower room,
Her father rubbing down his hands.

#### BURLEY

There towered an infant on her face!

#### JACK

And thereafter, all the sad forlorn.

#### AUGUSTA

Who are you that you know anything?

#### JACK

The crystal like a pregnant girl has hour
When it delivers up its oracle,
Leaving the chamber to the adversary.
The eye-baby now you're pregnant with
You'll carry in your iris to the grave.
You made yourself a *madam* by submission;
With, no doubt, your apron over-head,
And strewing salt all up and down the stairs
To catch whose feet? Hers alone, or his,
Walked that last mile? Miranda not yet seventeen.
Thrown to a travelling Cockney thrice her age,
Indeed Brigid-Matilda's brother. Why?
Titus had him handy for experiment;
Though Miranda cried first, like the ewe,
'Do not let him—but if my father wills it—!'
Offering up her silly throat for slashing,
Already bubbling in the lamentation.
So I say between you both you made
Of that doll's *abattoir* a babe's *bordel*.

#### AUGUSTA

[*Looking wildly about, and seeing stray travellers, who have climbed
up the back way into the gallery, staring down at her.* AUGUSTA
*throws herself over the doll's house, beating at it with both hands*]
Get them off! Enough! Stop it! Away!

Peepers! Histrions! Mountebanks! Retrievers!
Whatever trapper hunts me overhead—
Whistle off the nightingales and doves
Who fouled this house with their co-counsel moan!
Speed the footfall of the fox and hare;
Let from hence all beasts repair away;
All wings bend and outward fly; lest one proclaim
What this fearful haunt has seen!

[*All the heads disappear from the balcony.* MIRANDA *helps her mother down from the table, putting her own cloak about her.*]


MIRANDA

Come, come to supper.


AUGUSTA

How have my reflections gone from out
The pools of Burley. How I've fumbled my escape!

[*As all go towards the pantry,* ELISHA *gives* MIRANDA *the ass's head.*]


ELISHA

Miranda, I give you our weapons. Jack, to you
My compliments. You pulled a trick unseats us all.


BURLEY

[*Taking* AUGUSTA'S *arm*]

My arm, Augusta.


MIRANDA

[*Allowing all to pass in, detains* BURLEY, *who gives* AUGUSTA'S *arm to* DUDLEY]

A moment, Uncle.
For the rest I do absolve you of the company.
For your part in it, I thank you.
You've seen us shaken by diminutive
And brought down low, like Hector, by the heel;
But then of course, Hector is always dead.
Here is a rate too special for your years;
I ask you, be not present, be prevented.
As the ballerina on perfected toe

Spins to the axis of a fortitude
That is the sum of all her yesterdays,
So I to this lodestone of mine must turn.
In your spare fastidious alarm
I think you think to sit this session out.
Abjure it. You sit between two beasts in chancery
Who fight, head down, between them for a grave
That neither of them has a conduct for.
You, dear uncle, have a manner in yourself
So amenable to destiny, I love you for it.
But here is something more than monstrous wicked:
The spirit being chameleon to the mind
And that mind vulgar, I tell you be not present.
As a criminal in the wash of crime—
As a bell-buoy hauls the running tide
And rocks but in the leeway of the roll—
So my head voyages at tether in the blow.
Yet I do swear, dear uncle, I have loved
Three sons, and one woman, to the heart.


BURLEY

Sons?


MIRANDA

What else, if I am she, and she Miranda?


BURLEY

'A poet is a light and winged thing, and holy',
As Plato said. You are in the wash of such;
The which your people know; it is their cruel pleasure.


MIRANDA

[*With affection*]
If all the martyrs in the catacombs
Should take it in their heads to move away,
You'd compute the dissolution augury,
And just on chance you'd keep the dove-cote swept.
I think you must have heard the dead unpack
Their wings before, for here's a clapping air.
But no, not yet. This is a clocked encounter

To which I would not have you sacristan.
You are unfit for stumble in conformity—
And wonderfully is man made counterfeit.
Therefore, when you have supped, return
And help me make of this divided beast
An undivided bed.

[*Exit* BURLEY]


CURTAIN

# Act Three

*The gryphon has been brought together. The tented curtains of lace clubbed in the carnival crown. On this car* MIRANDA *lies sleeping.*

[AUGUSTA *enters, followed by* BURLEY, *carrying a lamp.*]

AUGUSTA

See, she has a sleep. I gave it her.
My hoard of me, remission, recompense.
See how she darkens; how compounds me.
But does she not breathe short of ransom?

BURLEY

[*To himself*]

In circus Vaticanus fallen.

AUGUSTA

It's terrible to walk behind old children, Jonathan,
Who once tipped back their heads to drink.

BURLEY

I think it time you saw her as Miranda.

AUGUSTA

I think it's time I saw me as Augusta.
There's the curfew-bell, and it's o'clock, and bedlam.
Shall I ring and wake her?

BURLEY

Do not wake her. There's a ligature in sleep
Binds us to waking; lease her.
Good night, Augusta.

AUGUSTA

Where are the boys?

99

BURLEY

Above you, resting in the gallery.

AUGUSTA

Good night, Jonathan.
And Jack?

BURLEY

For safety, with his horse.

MIRANDA

[*Waking*]
Is that you, Uncle?

BURLEY

Good night, my dear.

MIRANDA

Good night, Uncle.

[*Exit* BURLEY]

AUGUSTA

Good night.

[*Inspecting the gryphon*]
A solid beast, an excellent stage, fit for a play.

MIRANDA

To bed, to bed.

AUGUSTA

I think I have forgotten Beewick and the beast.

MIRANDA

I think it.

AUGUSTA

Will you stay?

MIRANDA

That depends.

On what?

MIRANDA
                    On many things.

AUGUSTA
You have it very pleasant here.

MIRANDA
So travellers say—of other people's stations.

AUGUSTA
So, let us play. The epilogue is over,
The boys asleep, and we are girls again
Nor need not think of them this part of night.
When you were young and out of company
I made you sitting donkeys, one like that
But only smaller. I made you ducks and drakes
Of butter-coloured flannel and stocking legs.
        [*She mounts the bed, facing* MIRANDA]
My amends—for every kind of thing.
Now the animals are put up in their box,
Let us be young again and tell us of our lives.
Recount to me, Miranda, who have been too slain
In public, how it is. What news of me?

MIRANDA
Looking down the twilight of your eye
I see the body of a bloody Cinderella
Come whirling up its caustic bore.

AUGUSTA
My last of two worlds, my trick of tricks;
My ace in hole—comes flying up with me!
Come, play me daughter.

MIRANDA
Hold, woman!
There was a time when we were not related.
When I first loved thee— I say 'thee' as if

It were to use a lost endearment
That in the loss has lost the losing world—
When I first loved thee, thou wert grazing:
Carrion Eve, in the green stool, wading:
In the coarse lilies and the sombre wood;
Before the tree was in the cross, the cradle, and the coffin,
The tragic head-board, and the victim door,
The weeper's banister, the cunning panel.
When yet the salt unspilt, the bread unbroken,
The milk unquested, uncried and unsprung,
You came braying for a victim lover.
The cock crew, the spur struck, and Titus Adam
Had at you with his raping-hook
And you reared back, a belly full of thumbs.

AUGUSTA

By my heaven, that was my greenest sickness!
I was slumming when I let you wear my belly.

MIRANDA

Have it so. Then began the trick of tricks,
The balking embryo. That mischief's parcel,
That legless flight, that gizzard brain,
That sitting hummock crouching on the head,
Computing its slow minting inch, that orphan,
Purblind, faceless, jellied in its course,
Rolling in a palm-full of the belly's Thames,
A dockless hawser 'round about its neck,
Praying without hands—lolled on its thumb,
And time commenced.

AUGUSTA
[*Frightened—but without gesture*]
                                          Shssssh!

MIRANDA

The salt spilled, the bread broke. Unmuzzled bone
Drew down the hood of flesh, entombing laughter:
Tongues came forth, and forth the hissing milk
Its lashing noose, and snared the gaping mouth.

102

A door slammed on Eden, and the Second Gate,
And I walked down your leg.

AUGUSTA

Alas, your father!

MIRANDA

Alas, my mother!
I would his groin had been as shadowless
As Origen's ere I had rustled in his lap.

AUGUSTA

What's here!

MIRANDA

What's not here!

AUGUSTA

To think I have a daughter for Inquisitor!

MIRANDA

To think I had a mother should betray me!
Tax me guilty both of audit and default;
Tot me up, as idiots their droppings,
And as indifferently, tick off the count.

AUGUSTA

What has wrought you to this sudden fury?

MIRANDA

What? Thinking on the shoddy lamentation
Rung about so desolate a journey.
Only yesterday, the heaped up chronicle—
Where you crossed your palms upon your gown
To guard the secret of the belly's botany—
Was grappled by my father's bloodhound hand
And I ripped public for the scapegoat's run.

AUGUSTA

[*Knuckle to eye*]
Love is death, Miranda. I am tame
As I'm forgotten.

103

MIRANDA
                              Even the frightened die.

AUGUSTA
Oh, think of it!


MIRANDA
Love is death, and death is maidenly.
It wrestles in the brasses and the rods
Of whatsoever trestle love lies on.
What else but murder with the mackerel eye
Couples with the tenants of that bed?
Crying 'I love, I hunger and I fear!'
With arms and legs stuck forthright as the slain
Under the bloody linen of the butcher's cart.
So I say with Pericles
'Murder's as near to lust as flame to smoke'.

AUGUSTA
Let's not talk of irremediable things,
Let's talk of me.
Could I love again?

MIRANDA
Does the fallen drummer-boy, his heel
In muscular contraction, kick his drum?

AUGUSTA
You are too old for me, and merciless.
You who never were revengeful are become so.

MIRANDA
Not revengeful, but much another thing.

AUGUSTA
Let's jump the Day of Wrath. Let us pretend.
The play is over and the boys are put to bed.
Let's play at being Miranda and Augusta.
Say we're at some hunting box with lords—
Say duck sniping—on a lake, or snaring
Woodcock in the hills—shooting and kissing—
Your father wore the trappings, but his aim was wild.

MIRANDA

So it was.

AUGUSTA

So then let us forget him.
I think the gryphon moved. We have a carriage!
Let's go to Ostend, Monte Carlo, Brighton;
The Lido, Palm Beach, Breisgau, Carcassonne—
And don't forget the flares and chandeliers—
The pleasure gardens, Vauxhall, Fontainbleau,
The Trianon, and fountains, and the music!

MIRANDA

[*Smiling*]
No fountains—no flambeaux, no music nor no gallants.

AUGUSTA

Then on to Longchamp, Ascot, Aintree, Epsom!
Regattas, fairs; horse racing in the Corso?
Anything. Bartholomews. Let's catch
A fairing at a stall; let's dance a jig.
Let's to Billingsgate with fife and drum!

MIRANDA

Have you forgotten Calvin?

AUGUSTA

I'll sit in a supper box with Richelieu—
But later. Now we're off for Maxime's, only
Call in the caterers, the pigeons, larks and torches;
Let us join the gentlemen!
    [*Without asking permission,* AUGUSTA *takes off* MIRANDA'S *shoes,
    puts them on her own feet, and in exchange puts her slippers on*
    MIRANDA]
Love puts forth her foot; let's to the opera.

MIRANDA

Love puts forth her foot, and in my shoes.

AUGUSTA

[*Holding up her hand*]
Look! Lying fallow at death's door these many days

I have me back my pleasant foot and hand,
The hand as seemly white as any unemployed,
The ankle small and fit.
So I'll to the hunting lodge of Meyerling.
I'll romp me in an hide-away in Garmisch.
Or shall I be a Tuscan with strict flanks
Stomping, to a singer from Auvergne?
Or a Gascon?

MIRANDA
No.

AUGUSTA
No?
Then have it I am Empress Josephine,
With an hat full of Napoleon's bees;
Some chief imprudent of the *haute noblesse*—
Or no, Lily Langtry, tipping glass of sorbet,
Waiting on the inert Prince of Somewhere
To pitch it down the pathway to his seat!
And don't forget the pinwheels and the rockets!

MIRANDA
O delayed and waiting creature.

AUGUSTA
Could you say I'd seen the baths of Caracalla?
Tickled from the keel of Lost Atlantis
All her drowned crustacean lovers bobbing
That great city, that ocean-going crab?
Or have I been a Tudor crone, sea-hag, for nothing?
Have I ruffled, in all, the golden hen
But to set sour eggs before foul gentlemen?

MIRANDA
I fear it.

AUGUSTA
What! Are you too *young* for me, indeed?
Was I ever princess in a legend?
   [*Whispers*]
*Did I sleep a hundred years?*

MIRANDA

Mother, there's no more time. All's done.

AUGUSTA

[*In a frantic whisper*] *Was I stolen?*

MIRANDA

O unhappy wanderer—
I've seen you dig for Antony
With a kitchen spoon.

AUGUSTA

[*Pretending to check*]
Was I Svengali's evening thrush? Delsarte's
Best equation? Did I lean on Persian?
[*She takes on a most affected pose*]
With the first finger held up for the finches:
The left hand poised upon the right hand's back,
Gum-arabic curbing the restless laces,
[*Dropping the pose*]
Jess to the wrist? Or was I in the gallery
The day the guillotine was shucking heads?
Was it I who, dipping kerchief at Antoine,
Came up with Augusta on my napkin?
O Miranda, staunch me!

MIRANDA

Do not press so hard upon the point.

AUGUSTA

Never walked beside the Serpentine?
Never checked a victor's knobs and bosses
On any field of any Marathon?
Nor never, in great joy, kissed on the mouth
By a mouth deposed between me and the kissing?
I've too much nature in me, daughter,
And you too old.

MIRANDA

Ah, that mouth with cutlass in the gape
To cut you down from the forbidden tree.
Dearest, worst and sorriest, had been a man
You'd been the bloodiest villain of us all.

107

[*Grinning*]
Why then I am!
But you blow my candle out, could read
With your bare eyes a dead man back again.
Do not vote me of that dateless herd
Lowing without tongue—huge freight of silence—
On a frieze ten pastures down,
But pull me up as we had high carouse;
I'll willing be a transient to this world
And it be Now—and jollity!
Or is gone all pride and merriment?
Shall I have no gales, nor games, nor country pleasures,
'Where'er I walk?' but 'crowd into a shade'?
Not scattered in the bloom, but as the wrack,
Sea-grape, its bladders and full bush
A bramble off the banks, and kicked by wind and rain?
Not gathered in the hunting hand, not sleeked,
Not prospered, tended, wholly desolate?
Take mercy on my prentice cries, Miranda,
Leave me not so sharp, unsung, and shrill;
With autumn's savage jet my bosom brooked,
My harvest awn all down, and leaning on my hand.
The once new-risen loaves of my brimmed breast
Kissed in the busk; now bowling low in sag
Knock their withered acorns on my knee:
So, the phoenix runs upon her ashes!

MIRANDA
O mother, mother!

AUGUSTA
You call this wisdom? I call it winter!
Where *are* the banquets and the cavaliers?
How near to my last travesty your spading foot?
Am I soon cargo of that creeping thing
Whose very texture is the inside-kissing lip?
'Man owes a death to God', you say? So be it.
But if there is no God, then God forgive him!
You too are grown unkind with shivering.
Allay my sorrow then, you cruel girl;

Medicine me to some account more just;
Do not so fumble my futurity.

MIRANDA

Blow less hard about the stage. Be still.

AUGUSTA

Then absolve me of the mischief is Augusta.
Snatch me out. I come on me in vain.

MIRANDA

The thing that's touched is sacked. Stand.

AUGUSTA

You won't even tell me how you are, or what.

MIRANDA

Trappist—sprung—and of an hard-won silence.

AUGUSTA

Nothing else about your history?

MIRANDA
                    Nothing.

AUGUSTA
                    Nothing at all?

MIRANDA
                    Nothing at all.

AUGUSTA
   [*Taking up* MIRANDA'S *hat*)
So then. Like a Norman widow, having hung—
Speaking in metaphor—your father's hat
Upon its proper post, may I have yours?
   (*She puts on* MIRANDA'S *hat*)
My daughter is winged serpent, *and* the urn.
Some damned dark Beatitude that sits
In her heart's core, mewling like an idiot,
Cribs her out of eminence and profit;

109

Sweeps her from the kingdom and the general world—
And she sits by and strokes its bloody head.

MIRANDA
Observant. . . .

AUGUSTA
I'm swan-sick, girl, and more than tired of roses.
Give me then my thistles and my thorn;
The un-may'd daisies' harsh and scentless spring,
And all the weeds that of no summer wane.
The castor, spurge, the bitter root and hazel;
My short hand-bloom, my borage and my stock.
You gave me myrtles yesterday, you say?
But I live from hour to hour—and it is past.
Give me your hand in absence: part in meeting:
You who should have been the first born of the two.

MIRANDA
There's a cry of women!

AUGUSTA
[*Leaning forward, in an urgent whisper*]
Is it true that you had forty lovers?

MIRANDA
Bridge of asses! Would you cross on me?
So it's I you stung for winter feast?

AUGUSTA
[*Covering her face*]
Do not leave me drenching in my hands.
Do not stamp me down for tally in the earth,
The 'lo, behold!' of raveners. Be merciful.
When this body drops from off this ghost
Who'll bell that cat?

MIRANDA
[*Uncovering* AUGUSTA'S *face*]
What! not weeping after all! I had suspected it.
There are, they say, strange cattle in a tear

110

Go on another business than our own;
And grazing, pull our sorrow up.

AUGUSTA

It's not I wouldn't, it is that I cannot.
My natural showers have wept unnatural moons.
I'm grinned away, to catch my sons' attention.

MIRANDA

I sorrow you've been too much blamed for praise.
Yet who knows, when Oedipus grubbed out
The luggage of his sight upon a pin,
For what in-caverned vision then he mined?
They say he who digs far down for love
Brings up the brightest burning coal.
Be not your own pathetic fallacy, but be
Your own dark measure in the vein,
For we're about a tragic business, mother.

AUGUSTA

Who *are your* people?

MIRANDA

By the unrecording humours of my eye
It should be observed I have no people:
But on the dark side, there I entertain.

AUGUSTA

Then tell me, how the movement of the bowels?

MIRANDA

What stroke is that?

AUGUSTA

I like to keep in touch with my posterity.

MIRANDA

It has been remarked from advent to the terror
Woman is most beast familiar.

III

AUGUSTA

[*Grinning*]

Then give me news of something fabulous—
What? No news of that?

MIRANDA

No news of that.

AUGUSTA

No man died for you?
Nothing? No news of famous people?

MIRANDA

No famous people, and no man died.

AUGUSTA

Willow, willow, willow!
If you won't make the either of us notable,
Or put us on the index of The Book,
Then put us near to someone who's been near it.
There was Fenimore Cooper's house, and Poe's.
I myself was once asked to a garden party—
Archbishop Benson's. Just behind the close.
They saw me sitting up. Say 'Who *is* Sylvia
That all the swains adore her?'

MIRANDA

Indeed, who.

AUGUSTA

I've not been loved enough to be forgotten.
I am too old to be so frightened, daughter,
And unreliable with sorrow. Tell me—
You who are for ever somewhat blunt,
And I where now no salt can catch me—
Tell me, was there a woman, once *so* well beloved
She yet lies still beneath a ton in India,
With reasonable hands?

MIRANDA

She does.

## AUGUSTA

And did a legend under-sea break water
To leap into a lover's lap?

## MIRANDA

She did.

## AUGUSTA

See?
I believe more things than I believe,
So I try to remember who I am tomorrow,
For I don't believe in anything today.
Fie! this striving, fancying, believing!
I have, I say, small patience with the mind
That dares oblivion and peoples it
With such cranks of heart. I would be Helen,
Forgotten for forever and forever
By each several recalling generation
Throughout eternal times succeeding.
Fie! I say, upon the whole of love's debris;
That horrid holocaust that is the price
Of passion's seizure. Why, I've even heard
That insects shed, and birds in copulation, moult;
That in some kind the very beaks are wrung
And scattered all about the forest floor.
I've been told of boys, come to majority,
Their baby mittens yet fast hot upon them
That later, in the doff of rite, were found
Wristless, unhanding a cooling bed.

## MIRANDA

I wonder is there any instrument,
Beside harmonica, a man, a comb,
Plays full gamut to the indrawn breath?

## AUGUSTA

There's a choir of howlers in the middle air
That only our others hear. Your father's hound
The smallest basset, loosed on Exeter
High on the leads, flushed out a vicar
Not at that point assembled in the womb.

H                    113

MIRANDA

I wonder what it is that madmen hear
Calls them on crusade that is a cheat.


AUGUSTA

If you are speaking of your father, I forgive him;
I've younger men are walking 'round my mind.


MIRANDA

[*More to herself than to Augusta*]
Titus! Self-appointed Holy Ghost and Father.
Prophet, Saviour, out of Salem—brag of Heaven;
Wived in righteous plenty—Solomon.
Got himself precisely where he quailed,
All his abrogations skive-side in;
And in his fancy twice as dedicate as Stephen,
That crusading infant, and so like him
No sooner got a following than impudence;
And hoist upon the shoulders of his children
Rode, shaking his rattle over Pendry,
Crying, 'Down with the schoolroom, church, and king!'
And to lay that tower of dust, his first-born's tears.


AUGUSTA

Then the law, the fright, the recantation—


MIRANDA

And all his sons fell to the market-place
Of a world's already planned destruction,
His heel upon their heads.


AUGUSTA

[*Sweetly*] So were we all betrayed.


MIRANDA

Where man lauds himself abroad, and blows
So full a gale of women all before him,
What interdiction saves?
He who, for fear, denies the called response
Denies the singing and damns the congregation.
I've often wondered how so many women
Managed to hod so many children on one boast.

114

AUGUSTA

                I said you are a wicked woman.


MIRANDA

I know, the last time was the last time that you saw me.
That was another war, when all of you
Knowing I had nothing but myself
And my book, you sold that to my brother
Who grinned, as though I had been bought.


AUGUSTA

May God protect us! I wonder what you'll write
When I am dead and gone.


MIRANDA

My brother said, 'Break her, who is not altar broken,
That's the way to catch her, and throw the key away
And leave her, like a maniac in a cell,
Combing the tousled visions in her mind,
Dreaming a dream no man can tell.' And you?
Why mother, they'd have had you by the scruff
Still in appetite, in sense, and quaking cold,
And thrown you to the gammers of the pit—
Except I put my foot against that door.


AUGUSTA

You almost amounted—once. I've said it.


MIRANDA

    [*With bitterness*]
But, by my heaven, not the money-wink?
That drawbridge to a safe economy,
That hooded glare the condor turns on quarry,
The eyelid that absolves him of the kill.


AUGUSTA

                Who are you become?


MIRANDA

Have I not said it?
One of a strolling company of players.

Say wardrobe mistress, tiring many parts.
You see yourself, you have my rings and boots,
My cloak and hat.

  [*Back to pleasant thoughts*]
So I have!
Buckled shoes and rings, and feathered hat!
Do let's pretend we're girls again; let's play.
If dull at home, one may be skilled abroad.
There must be ways to catch a world.


MIRANDA
Ah, yes. Every mother, in extortion for her milk—
With the keyhole iris of the cat—draws blood.
Teasing the terror for the teasing story,
And for what it's worth in foreign places temporal,
Applauding with kill-kindly tongue of charity
As of benchers in the last dispensary:
  [*With the tongue*]
'Tick, tick, mercy that one took her shifty life
In satin slippers! Only fancy!'


AUGUSTA
Major wind, blow less minor daughter!
I'd have you smaller—though cast up for glory—
Somewhat lower down, where I can catch you!


MIRANDA
That's more like it. Then let us speak of men,
And the quality in that I am recalled by.
Let us say a burgomaster up in Üffing
Unseats me every time he goes to funeral,
Or when, raising his top-hat at weddings
He finds me nesting in the lining of his gibus,
In the shape of one small rabbit toque.


AUGUSTA
I like that! I like to think you're honoured
Even at the bottom of a hat.

116

MIRANDA

If splendid folly is your appetite
And sly Islamic humour to your taste,
Then say a Berber of the Atlas left me
One hundred horses.

AUGUSTA

Because you had no seat?

MIRANDA

Because I had no stable.

AUGUSTA

[*Rising*]
Daughter,
There's a battlement in every woman's heart
Whereon she keeps perpetual patrol
To scape the man she married, for that man
Heard scratching in the wall.

MIRANDA

Till through some aperture in desolation
The ticking lover-beetle creeps?

AUGUSTA

Think of it.
All through my beauty he enjoyed an ugly woman!
That man your father. I said his acts to me
Were never gentle, fond nor kind;
Nor he never held nor stroked me anywhere;
And you stood up, as in a lost equation,
As you had mended such economy.

MIRANDA

And so I should indeed, had I been able,
But metempsychosis not for asking:
And between us stands the argument.

AUGUSTA

I knew that you'd say nothing comforting.
Yet I swear the Virgin did not love

Her chirrup more than I my children.
*Make me something!*

MIRANDA

Largo, largo! Hold your rate in ordinary!
Do not confuse the advent with assumption.
Nor at this starve, go throw me up for target.
The wind that knocked our generation down
Was not an harvest.
The Queen of Heaven, holding trust ajar
For the entrance and the exit of Good News
Was nothing similar.

AUGUSTA

Of course you always have it your own way;
You're the terrier runs back without the bone.

MIRANDA

How is it that women who love children
So often damn the children that they have?
Would you propose a beggared silk-worm draw
From out her haggard poke so brave a silk
Could card a paragon?

AUGUSTA

Ah, failed!

MIRANDA

Rebuke me less, for we are face to face
With the fadged up ends of discontent:
But tie and hold us in that dear estrangement
That we may like before we too much lose us.
As the goldsmith hammers out his savage metal,
So is the infant axial to the dance.
Wrapped in metric; hugged in discipline,
Rehearsed in familiarity reproved;
Grappled in the mortise of the ritual,
Turning on the spirit of the play—
Equilibrium else would be a fall,
Paid for in estrangement, each from each.

118

## AUGUSTA

Magpie! With my world wrapped in a napkin!
In what pocket have you my identity?
I so disoccur in every quarter of myself
I cannot find me;
Suttee to an ember burning cold.
In your valid and unshaken company
I still dangle for the cockatrice
My unsucked eggs.

## MIRANDA

Where the martyr'd wild fowl fly the portal
High in the honey of cathedral walls,
There is the purchase, governance and mercy.
Where careful sorrow and observed compline
Sweat their gums and mastics to the hive
Of whatsoever stall the head's heaved in—
There is the amber. As the high plucked banks
Of the viola rend out the unplucked strings below—
There is the antiphon.
I've seen loves so eat each other's mouth
Till that the common clamour, co-intwined,
Wrung out the hidden singing in the tongue
Its chaste economy—there is the adoration.
So the day, day fit for dying in
Is the plucked accord.

## AUGUSTA

And how am I, in this kingfisher night,
To brim me to the brim and stay uncaught?
My calendar is hulled, my lands in plague;
The locust, jacket-jumped, claws to my stile
So we stare on each the other with unbuttoned eyes
In such abandoned case as kills the heart.
Would you call a plague of absence, company?

## MIRANDA

Yes.

## AUGUSTA

So the haggard cries in vain 'Whoa!' to the drover.
We admire each other in our cruel way.

Unpack your purse—afford me. But no matter;
After all, what can you say you've saved?

MIRANDA
The loss.

AUGUSTA
What does that mean? Never mind that either.
When I'm dead and gone, put me to a tree.

MIRANDA
Presently.

AUGUSTA
Why don't you love us any more?
That is the question—
Where *is* Miranda?

MIRANDA
The question is, why do I? Where's Miranda?
Thugged to death, not killed upon the altar;
Carrion cast, not offering. Let's ask
Where is that coign and cupboard of the heart
That mothers used to keep their warbler in?
The gate's ajar, and the imp has flown,
Scotched by the sword her people snatched
From before the gate of Eden, for a whip
To beat her, staggering like an headless cock,
Ramshackle, aghast, and staring all abroad—
A gaze contained in nothing.
What echoes swarmed that blind and bloody head?
The Dead Sea frog croaking in the hoof
Of a Dead Sea nun, running down the cloister.
Miranda, bushelled in the mind's confessional
Foxed down its gullet to the rump,
Quaking with unhouselled mouth; her tail
In flinders, like the wood-hen shaking,
Lashing at the lattice with her paws.

AUGUSTA
[*Lamely*]
Then you weren't saved, God save us, after all?

120

#### MIRANDA

Woman, I've seen my people set the canine tooth
Into the Host; I've heard them lapping at the wound.
What do you think?

#### AUGUSTA

God have mercy on me!

#### MIRANDA

God have mercy on us all; and may He
Forgive me my abominable innocence
That I can't think what it is I've done,
Who have not seen my people many years,
To so estrange us.

#### AUGUSTA

I want Jeremy; where is Jeremy?
God is so slow with me; where in my son?

#### MIRANDA

Where, indeed.

#### AUGUSTA

He would have stayed with me, if you had stayed.
He'd have wanted to, if you had wanted to;
You were both so fond of each the other;
He turned to you, but he couldn't stand it.

#### MIRANDA

What!
Would you I'd kept his mother's stalk upon him?
Dealt him a pack of tricks, cut by his sister,
In a deal that had not counted him?
Neither juried, judged, verdict'd nor dismissed,
But in stound, with mouth too tender for the hook?
Why, what a thing, and how he would have plunged!

#### AUGUSTA

Gone, gone! cast out and waning
Like a circle running from a stone
Pitched upon a frightful deed; forgotten.
I leave the whole catch to the resurrection!

121

Do you?
Do you think there'll be no tussle in that trench?
And would you set this vile doll up again?
You who would un-breath my dying breath
From off the tell-tale mirror plate
To blow into the furnace of his mouth,
Haggling in a market place.
Why, at the first trump of impending Doom
You'll come roaring up the galleys of the dead,
The oar-arms banked and trussed upon the bone,
Crying 'J'accuse!' and hale me by the browse
And in alarm bark out 'Not this arouse!
Guilt has her, let guilt haul her house!'
Beating your belly's cage where I took stroke;
Running halt, distracted, and about;
Counting which of my hairs be summoned at the root.

AUGUSTA
Mother of God!

MIRANDA
Precisely not.

[*Both women are now at the foot of the stairs.* MIRANDA *fending, with her skirts fanned wide,* AUGUSTA *following.*]

AUGUSTA
Something's wrong. Where is my Jeremy?
I will catch my son!

[*They begin to mount*]

MIRANDA
Key-gone generation. The figured base
So many scattered minims on the wind,
All to amuse a frightened man, his generation;
And astound one woman of great folly.

AUGUSTA
Don't tell me there's nothing hereabout.
You, who've always been too fond of death,
Will soon be as nothing as your mother!

MIRANDA

Ah, the gauntlet in the gift!
I've always been obliged to death, indeed.
It is the rate in everything I do.
It is the matter that I turn upon.
It is the hub that holds the staggered spindle.
It is the plumb-bob, piddock, gravity
Of the Surveyor with the cautious hand:
A portion of man's dignity, he dies.

AUGUSTA

Don't tell me anything again!
I've heard the cry of hunter, 'Gone away!'
And the howl of 'Wolf!' The cry of man, that too.
I know you'd have me Tudor Crone, undone.
I tire of all the downward obsequies,
Lauds, canticles, requiems and masses;
The upraised finger pointing zero.

MIRANDA

The frantic sloth of grieving, the hidden head—
By its waters eaten. The high crossed sleeves;
The muffled drum, the creeping catafalque
Toiling backward to the cot; the great stone fly
Sarcophagus, at flemish in the ways—

AUGUSTA

The excellent arrangement of catastrophe;
The nice matter of the closed account!

MIRANDA

Perambulator triumphant to the tomb—
Death with a baby in its mouth. Procession
Turning arc-wise to the turning cradle:
The plumed mares, with the sea-salt heavy tassels.

AUGUSTA

The pomp and circumstance of childhood, driven
By an headless coachman, whistling—

123

MIRANDA

'Who passes by this road so late?'

AUGUSTA

What's that?
Are you trying to frighten me?

MIRANDA

No, trying to make us fit to be forgotten.

AUGUSTA

You are frightening me. Where is my youth?

MIRANDA

At this moment, bent down to greet your shadow,
Running on all fours to keep you company.

AUGUSTA

[*Pushing at* MIRANDA]
Let me go; I know your citizens of silence—
    [*Hearing* DUDLEY *and* ELISHA *making their escape*]
Out of my way, you tool of earth!
Should I cry now, whose cries were *always* swindled?
Let me go, I say!

MIRANDA

[*Trying to prevent* AUGUSTA *from reaching the top landing*]
Be not so swift to see and know.

AUGUSTA

[*Stopping short*]
Are you staying?

MIRANDA

I am staying.

AUGUSTA

Why?

MIRANDA

Is it really possible that you don't know

124

That your sons have come to hunt you down?
I was in the panel once before
When you were all but small bread in the basket
Undertakers rock before a quand'ry.
I heard my brothers move through price of pine
To the cheaper bargain—burning on a shovel.
Even then, reverberation of a coin
Spent in sorrow's haste so shook their being
That coursing the journey of that dole
Their hands trembled half a day. You have such sons
Would mate the pennies on a dead man's eyes
To breed the sexton's fee.

> [*At this point the departure of* DUDLEY *and* ELISHA *is only too clearly audible.* MIRANDA *and* AUGUSTA *having reached the other side of the landing, now descend in the order in which they mounted,* MIRANDA *still fending with her outspread skirts.*]

AUGUSTA

Out of my way! I think my sons have left me!

MIRANDA

      Stay with me. They left you long ago.

AUGUSTA

Stay? What, in this place, and uninhabited?
*No!*

MIRANDA

Yes.
They chased you home to lose you.
This is your habit, they the lost account;
Citizens without a people in the blood,
Nor even ride a saddle they have stitched.
Your grave is also on a journey; join it:
Save your death.

AUGUSTA

No! Yes. They call me hermit-crab, and shut
The orifices of the heart, lest I crawl in.
    [*Given pause*]
Man, by its titter underground, finds gold,

125

And with what passion does he dig it up!
But let it be the heavy mother lode,
With what passion will he dig her in!

MIRANDA

Then stay with me and uncle Jonathan
And do as I.
Caught in the utmost meridian and parallel—
As of a moor-hen, watching a hawk heel in,—
Draw 'round in dust the broken wing
Its last veronica.

[MIRANDA *and* AUGUSTA *are now at the foot of the stairs. A sudden derisive blast of the car-horn announces the departure of* DUDLEY *and* ELISHA. *Hearing it,* AUGUSTA *seizes the curfew-bell, beating about* MIRANDA *its loud toll.*]

AUGUSTA

Stop them! Stop them! *You* let them get away!
It's your fault! You—you—you!

MIRANDA

[*Fending*] Wait. I'll be kinder later.

AUGUSTA

I know you. You are the one would lay
Me ticking down, ten cities deep!

MIRANDA

Nay, sparrow.
I'd lay you in the journey of your bed,
And un-bed you, and I could, in paradise.

AUGUSTA

Then why did you let me grow so old?
And let them get away—and Jeremy?
You are to blame, to blame, you are to blame—
Lost—lost—

[AUGUSTA *brings the ringing bell down on* MIRANDA. *Both fall across the gryphon, pulling down the curtains, gilt crown and all. The ringing ceases.* BURLEY *appears on the balcony, carrying a lamp.* JACK *turns in from the fallen portion of the wall.*]

126

BURLEY

What's done, Jeremy?

JACK

Ah, then Miranda knew. What's done?
Why, everything's done, uncle.

BURLEY

Both?

JACK

Both.
I might have known, being weary of the world,
And all the bootless roar of vindication,
She'd not defend herself. But could I know
Which would be brought to child-bed of the other?

BURLEY

Why did you do it?

JACK

Why? Do I carry the trefoil of the Cenci
That I should know what price the token price
That cashing in the utmost treasure would extort?
This is the hour of the uncreate;
The season of the sorrowless lamenting:
Say then, 'Jeremy, thou fool—thou soul of no abiding!'
As the criminal, snuffling 'round the kill,
Breathing his contagion out before him,
Draws up the victim with his steaming nose—
So I, who thought to medicine contumely
With a doll's hutch—that catches villains!—
Find I've breathed up my disaster and myself.
Say I was a man, of home so utterly bereft
I dug me one, and pushed my terror in.
Stand back, uncle.

[BURLEY *watches in silence as* JACK, *with what appears to be indifference, leaves the stage.*]

CURTAIN